P9-BXV-991

THE

TEN

COMMANDMENTS

To order additional copies of
The Ten Commandments,
by
Loron Wade,
call
1-800-765-6955.

Visit us at
www.reviewandherald.com
for information on other
Review and Herald® products.

THE

TEN

COMMANDMENTS

LORON WADE

REVIEW AND HERALD® PUBLISHING ASSOCIATION
HAGERSTOWN, MD 21740

Copyright © 2006 by
Review and Herald® Publishing Association
All rights reserved

The Review and Herald® Publishing Association publishes biblically
based materials for spiritual, physical, and mental growth and
Christian discipleship.

The author assumes full responsibility for the accuracy
of all facts and quotations as cited in this book.

Unless otherwise indicated, Scripture quotations in this book
are from the *New American Standard Bible,* copyright © 1960, 1962,
1968, 1971, 1972, 1973, 1975, 1977, 1994 by the Lockman
Foundation. Used by permission.

Texts credited to KJV are from the King James Version.

Texts credited to NKJV are from the New King James
Version. Copyright © 1979, 1980, 1982 by Thomas Nelson, Inc.
Used by permission. All rights reserved.

Bible texts credited to RSV are from the Revised Standard
Version of the Bible, copyright © 1946, 1952, 1971, by the Division
of Christian Education of the National Council of the Churches of
Christ in the U.S.A. Used by permission.

Bible texts credited to TEV are from the *Good News Bible*—
Old Testament: Copyright © American Bible society 1976, 1992;
New Testament: Copyright © American Bible Society 1966, 1971,
1976, 1992.

This book was
Edited by Gerald Wheeler
Copyedited by James Cavil
Cover designed by Trent Truman
Cover art by Harry Anderson (digitally modified)
Typeset: 11/13 Bembo

PRINTED IN U.S.A.

10 09 08 07 06   5 4 3 2 1

R&H Cataloging Service
Wade, Loron
  The Ten Commandments: what if we did it God's way?

  1. Ten commandments. I. Title.

241.52

ISBN 10: 0-8280-1999-1
ISBN 13: 978-0-8280-1999-6

CONTENTS

An Invitation
and a Promise

How would you draw the face of the world? I mean, if you wanted to describe the condition of the planet with a face, would it be a smiley? Or would it look worried, or afraid, or maybe even angry?"

We were meeting with some friends in their home in Costa Rica when I asked them this question.

"Well, I think—" Francisco started to give his opinion.

But just then something interrupted his words, and we never did find out what he was going to say. Our friends' home was in a long row of simple wooden houses. Each unit shared its walls with the neighbors. As a result, whatever went on in one house could pretty much get heard by the people on either side.

And while we were discussing the condition of the world, one of the neighbors came home. Slamming the door, he started yelling at his wife. It was obvious that he had been drinking, and his voice got louder and louder as he demanded something. I no longer recall what it was, but it was something she didn't have. And because she didn't hand it over instantly, he decided to exercise his manly authority by beating her up.

"I'm going to teach you to respect me," he shouted.

Above the terrific din of blows and screaming we could hear the voice of a little boy pleading and crying: "No, Daddy. No-o-o-o! Don't hurt Mommy. Please, please, don't hurt her."

You are probably reading this in a safe and peaceful environment. Is anyone yelling at you, or threatening to beat you? Probably not. So how would you draw the face of the world? Would you give it a really big smile?

Perhaps you may even thinking that I am using an extreme example here, not an illustration of how things really are. You notice I said this happened in Costa Rica, so that's OK, especially if you don't live there, because this is the sort of thing that always happens a long time ago and a long way from here. How many women do you think are being beaten up right now as you read this? In the United States it occurs every 15 seconds. How often do you think it happens in the rest of the world?

I am using domestic violence as an example of how things are in the world today. But I could employ countless other illustrations. How many people do you think are looking in a dumpster or in a landfill right now, hoping to find something to eat? Do you know what is the number one cause of infant death in the world is? Hunger. The World Health Organization reports that 5 million children die every year from causes related to malnutrition. That comes out to 13,700 every day. The monthly figure is a number that is more than all the people who died in the terrible seaquake and tsunamis of 2004.

Consider another example. How many people do you think are homeless? I'm not talking about the ones who got that way because of alcohol or igno-rance—only those whose lives have been torn apart by war and ethnic violence. The United Nations High Command for Refugees has, under its care, an estimated 20 million people who are either fleeing or living in extremely insecure conditions.

And, speaking of children, how many sleep every night on the streets in the great urban centers of the world, with nothing more than the cold pavement for a bed? No one knows the exact number, but UNICEF believes it is around 100 million, and the number is growing rapidly as a result of the AIDS epidemic. And a large percentage of them will become victims of abuse, addictions, and STDs, and many (or perhaps most) of them will become delinquents.

Napoleon supposedly observed that in war, God is always on the side of those who have the biggest guns. Today he would probably not say that, because terrorists depend not on cannons but on stealth and treachery. And now in many places they have joined forces with the drug barons, who seem to move freely across borders and only once in a while find them-selves challenged by the forces of law and order.

For a number of years it appeared as if penicillin was winning the war on social diseases—but that was before AIDS. The disease infects at least 45 million people today. It is wiping out a large portion of the population of sub-Saharan Africa and spreading rapidly everywhere else.

Think about it again: How would you draw the face of the world?

The strategy we use most often to isolate ourselves from so much suffering is massification. We avoid the pain by visualizing those suffering from such problems as faceless masses rather than as individuals. The other day a bomb went off in the Middle East. But I have never met Mustafa, one of the victims, and I wasn't there when it happened. I didn't try to help him while, choking with dust, he tore desperately through the rubble of his home until he found the body of his sister, the timid and gentle Hannah. My tears didn't flow while Mustafa beat his fists on the ground and moaned in anguish beside her mangled form.

It is easy to talk about tragedies. They happen, of course, but it wasn't my sister who died. A woman gets beaten up every 15 seconds? Yes, but I don't feel the blows, so I simply convert the experience into a statistic.

But the time is coming, and it is not far off, when this distancing strategy will no longer work. Because the storm that is breaking on our planet is growing in intensity, and already it is starting to reach into the private world of every human being. A generation ago we heard about drug addicts, but who knew one personally? Now everyone recognizes that tomorrow it may be my son who is a victim, or my daughter who gets an abortion. The attack on the twin towers was a wake-up call like nothing else in history. Who does not realize that today we are all vulnerable?

Sensationalists—people who go around with a message of doom written on sandwich boards—have always worried about the condition of the world. Now it is the soberest and best-informed people who are concerned. Fifty years ago philosophers began talking about "existential angst." Back then it was the private property of a few intellectuals. But that is no longer true today.

Efforts to Find a Solution

The nineteenth century was a time of optimism

unequaled in history. It was the heyday of rationalism, and people were convinced that the world was getting better and better. Technology offered countless wonders on almost a daily basis. Machines could now spin, weave, and sew. New inventions were transforming farming and industry. People could travel rapidly over land and sea, drawn by powerful steam engines. California learned about the death of Abraham Lincoln the same day it happened, thanks to the newly installed telegraph lines.

With all these wonders, people found it easy to believe that the problems of society would soon vanish. Poverty would disappear, and so would injustice, illness, and insanity. Wars would end in universal peace, and we would soon see the end of ignorance and tyranny.

But no longer. The golden age of optimism ended with World War I, and today it appears more of an illusion than ever. Science is racing ahead even faster now. But the hand that developed the transistor has also given us the atomic bomb and the ability to destroy civilization by pressing a button. And all over the world, people are asking: *With so much information, such amazing advances in understanding the universe, how is it possible that hunger, oppression, and tyranny still ride unchecked over the landscape?*

The problem is that we have tried to make science do a job it wasn't designed for. The reason such calamities go on year after year is that they are not scientific or technological problems.

Ask science how to project a ray of electromagnetic energy through space and send us a photo from the surface of Mars or Triton, and it will quickly give us the answer. Inquire how the human genome is organized, or what is the nature of endorphins and how they affect our brain cells, and it will not hesitate to answer. But if we ask it how to solve the worst problems of the age, it will have to say: *Sorry—that's not my area.*

This is because the worst problems of the age are not scientific but moral ones. Think about it a moment: Which of the great problems overwhelming society today is *not* a moral problem? They all are.

Take, for example, hunger. People are starving not because of a shortage of food in the world, but because of the terrible inequality of its distribution, which, in turn, is a result of the even more unequal distribution of wealth, education, and the means of production and transportation. The oppression and neglect of those who have nothing by those who have more than they need—what is it? It is definitely a moral problem.

And what about the other challenges and threats? Terror, political oppression, and tyranny are definitely moral situations. So are domestic violence, abortion, addiction, and the lifestyle that has made AIDS the greatest pandemic in history. If any of these were scientific or technological problems, we would have solved them long ago, because we are really good at that.

Some people may find it humiliating to accept what I am saying. They continue to cling to the foundation principle of rationalism—self-sufficiency. Its motto is: I can do it! My intelligence, my strength of character, my enterprising spirit, my whatever—but it is always me and my brains that are going to save the world. Such individuals refuse to admit that some problems do not have an intellectual solution.

This brings me to an important question: How much longer are we going to insist on looking in areas that cannot help us? How long will we continue knocking in panic on the doors of science when science is as frustrated as we are at its inability to offer any real or effective answers? How much more evidence has to slap us in the face before we accept the truth of this matter?

So What Is the Solution?

Faced with the obvious failure of science to do what it was never designed to do in the first place, should we simply resign ourselves to the status quo? Or is there a solution at hand that we have been overlooking for much too long?

If you ever have a chance to visit the Supreme Court building in Washington, D.C., when the Supreme Court is not in session, the tour guides will take you into the audience chamber where the nine justices hear the cases argued before them. Don't fail to raise your eyes a good deal above the bench and notice the figures carved in the frieze along the edge of the ceiling. Among the many figures there you will see an august-looking figure with stone tablets in his right hand. He is Moses, and the tablets he is holding are that ancient moral code known as the Ten Commandments.

Past generations, the ones who designed and built this great edifice, apparently did not suffer the same unjustified ego inflation that seems to afflict ours. They were willing to acknowledge the immense significance of this ancient law and its influence on society. Apparently they were not bothered by the fact that they had not invented it and that it was not a product of their own time.

Perhaps we find no better evidence of the spirit of our age—at least in the Western world—than the fact that certain activist groups today demand that such figures be removed from all public buildings.

And while this is going on, we are waiting, hoping against hope, that science will finally come up with a magic bullet to solve the impasse and get us out of our dilemma. It is precisely because of this insane egotism that things have come to the present state of crisis.

An Invitation and a Promise

Before going any further, I want to extend to you an invitation and also a promise:

I invite you to join me in considering the meaning of the moral law, that is, the Ten Commandments, for the twenty-first century. To do so, we will need to go beyond the surface and look at the powerful implications of these ancient principles, and consider their wisdom.

My promise is that this will not be a monologue. I don't plan to do all the talking. This is a discussion and study guide, and it is organized in a way that will encourage you be involved, to think for yourself, to interact and come to your own conclusions as we go along. You may even want to record your thoughts and do some journaling. I hope you do, because in the end my ideas or my conclusions about this are not the ones that will make a real difference in your life.

I said I was going to offer you a promise. Actually there are two, but the second one is part of the first one. It is this: I will never ask you to accept blindly anything I have to say about this extremely important subject. On the contrary, you will have ample opportunity to verify and prove for yourself the validity of the principles we are going to study.

This is possible because the Ten Commandments are not simply artifacts to be put on display somewhere in a glass case. A fountain flowing with practical wisdom, they offer real-time solutions to real problems and situations that all of us deal with every single day. They are principles that have a reasonable application in daily life, and their verification is in their application. The old-fashioned way of saying this is: "The proof of the pudding is in the eating."

As you test these principles in your life and make them a part of your world, you will know for sure that they are indeed valid, because the results will be immediate and deeply satisfying.

So don't hesitate. Step up and accept this invitation to study the Ten Commandments and make them a part of your life. You will be glad you did.

DANGEROUS LOVE

The First Commandment

You shall have no other gods before Me.
—Exodus 20:3

"You don't seem to get it, Jackie. It's your future that's at stake—your life!"

"No, Dad. You're the one who doesn't get it. It's been so long since you were young that you've forgotten what it was like. I'm telling you I *love* Danny. That's what you don't seem to understand."

Harry Williams stared unbelievingly at his daughter. Then with a sigh he shook his head, as if unable to comprehend what he was hearing.

"Jackie, you've got to listen to me."

"No! I'm not listening to anybody. I'm telling you, that's all. Next Tuesday the judge in the first civil court available downtown is going to marry us. Or maybe you want us just to go off and shack up?"

Another silence. Finally Harry spoke again, choosing his words carefully. "All right. I understand that it's your decision. No one is going to make you change your mind. I have just one question."

This time Jacqueline, happy that her father seemed to be respecting her right to choose, did not interrupt.

"Last Thursday you wore a white blouse when Daniel wanted you to wear a different one. How did he react?"

"Well, the blouse he wanted me to wear was stained. I'd spilled something on it."

"But my question is: What was your boyfriend's reaction? What did he say when he saw you in the white blouse?"

"Well . . . he wasn't exactly happy."

"Yes. In fact, he clenched his fist and yelled at you. And that same night, when we invited him to have dinner here at the house? What happened then?"

"Oh, Dad, never mind. It's over now. Why are you even bringing it up?"

"Because Danny didn't hesitate to embarrass you in front of the whole family when you said something he didn't like. Jacqueline, if that's how he treats you now, how do you think it will be when—"

"Stop it! Stop it!" she shrieked, clapping her hands over her ears. "Can't you understand? I love Danny. He is my whole life. Nothing else matters. What you're saying doesn't matter. What you think doesn't matter. I love him. I adore him. That's all that matters. Can't you understand?"

"You 'adore him'? You 'adore him,' Jacqueline? So what is Danny to you? Is he your god?"

"Sure, that's it. If that's how you want to say it, you're right. Danny is my god."

We will hit the pause button at this point and ask a question. Jacqueline's father told me later that those words stabbed like a knife into his heart. Do you believe he was being overly dramatic? Why do you think he felt such terrific anguish when he heard them?

Harry Williams trembled at his daughter's words because he knew the power that love has can hurt us and cause terrible damage. Love breaks through our shell and leaves us exposed and vulnerable as nothing else can.

Consider desperate parents waiting outside the intensive-care unit of a large modern hospital. Why are they feeling such intense anguish? It is because of love. And those same parents may be suffering just as intensely a few years later when this child comes home high on drugs.

How terrible it was for Jacqueline's parents, a few months later, when she began to reap the consequences of her terrible decision! With the fog of infatuation definitely blown away, she woke up to find herself united to a man who was intensely jealous and never satisfied with even her best efforts—who crushed her spirit with sarcasm, ridicule, and sometimes his fists! That is why Harry Williams trembled because of his daughter's attitude. He was terrified to see her place herself in the hands of someone who could hurt her so much.

And that is why God has given us the first commandment. It is a warning, offered out of deep concern. It means: *Don't surrender your loyalty and devotion to "gods" who in reality are no gods. Do not give a supreme place in your life to something or someone who, in the end, will only disappoint and hurt you.*

Failed Gods

The ancient people of Israel found themselves surrounded by nations who enthusiastically worshiped "other gods." There was Dagon, the chief deity of the Philistines, who were their neighbors to the west. The Philistines looked to him for good harvests and large catches of fish, which meant abundance and prosperity. The Phoenicians, Israel's neighbors to the north, were devoted to the moon goddess Ashtoreth, or Ashtart. She was in charge of fertility, and her worship was especially popular, because people celebrated it with drunken feasts and orgies. To the east, the Moabites worshipped Chemosh and the Ammonites Moloch. Both gods, especially the latter, accepted child sacrifices as ways to pacify and persuade them. The people went to such horrendous extremes hoping to enlist the power of these deities on their behalf.

Today, of course, popular culture has changed. Most people no longer bow down to gods of wood, stone, and metal. But money, sex, and power are still the driving forces in the lives of millions. The next time you go by a magazine stand, look at the covers and scan the titles. Notice the persistent themes of the talk shows and soap operas. What does this tell you about the "gods" that people worship most fervently today?

Then ask yourself: What has been the result, to date, of worshipping these "other gods"? Like the ones from long ago, they are also deities that turn against their worshippers and devour them.

From the frantic worship of sex has come the pandemic of AIDS. Why isn't anybody talking about the clearest and most obvious solution? It shouldn't be that hard to figure out. There is no need for this disease to spread further. The simplest, most obvious solution is to turn our backs on this treacherous deity and once again respect family values and the sacred character of marriage.

But instead of this, political leaders around the world are calling on their god "money" to save them. "Next year," they say, "we will spend still more millions. We will build bigger and better laboratories. Then we will find a vaccine so that you can continue with your lifestyle without fear of the consequences."

Terrorism has become the sword of the weak, the desperate recourse of the powerless. It feeds on fanaticism and ignorance, and finds its recruits in miserable refugee camps in which unhappy youth find themselves bombarded daily with the rhetoric of hatred.

And what is the solution proposed by those who find themselves under attack from such young fanatics? They are turning to the god "power": "We are going to build better rockets and bigger bombs. With them we will hunt those who oppress us, smoke them out, and crush them—that will solve our problems."

And what is the result of such a strategy? Every use of brute force strengthens the radicals in their sense of injustice and persecution. It creates still more anger and confirms their conviction that they are victims and that their hatred and violence are fully justified.

Don't surrender your loyalty and devotion to "gods" who in reality are no gods, says the first commandment. Do not give a supreme place in your life to something or someone who, in the end, will only disappoint and hurt you.

Failure of the Flowers

The New Testament tells us that one day Satan came to Jesus with an up-front, in-your-face attack on the first commandment. First he showed Him "all the kingdoms of the world and their glory," and then he said, "All these things I will give You, if You fall down and worship me" (Matthew 4:8, 9). *Here it is: money, sex, and power. You can have it all!*

But Jesus, in His reply, refused to focus on the false gods. Instead He turned the first commandment around and quoted Deuteronomy 10:20, which presents it in positive form: "It is written," He said: " 'You shall worship the Lord your God, and serve Him only' " (Matthew 4:10). Rejecting the false gods, denouncing their worship, is not enough. We must replace their worship with the worship of the God of heaven.

A generation ago "flower children," young men

and women with long hair and ragged clothing, filled the streets and parks of the Western world. Most people called them hippies. Hardly anybody today admires them. But we need to realize that they had a point. They were rejecting the false values of materialism. So why did their movement fail? It collapsed because they tried to take away without replacing. And in the end it was clear that they were simply exchanging one form of selfishness for another.

During those same years millions of people tried to implement the ideals of Communism, which, in its theoretical purity, advocates principles of sharing and unselfishness that sound a lot like the teachings of Jesus. Why did Communism fail to produce the ideal society it dreamed about? For the same reason. Like every other utopian vision, it shipwrecked on the rocks of human reality. It was based on the assumption that if you tell people they need to change, and if you can really convince them that they should, they will then change. But knowing what is right is not enough, and neither is just intellectually believing it.

In the 1970s Harvard psychologist Lawrence Kohlberg announced that he had found a way to make people more moral. His method was to ask people what was the right thing to do in certain hypothetical situations. He said he had succeeded in teaching them methods of moral reasoning so that they could come up with the right answer every time. But Kohlberg's theory got into trouble when someone thought to ask if knowing the right answer would actually result in anyone doing the right thing. The best answer he could come up with from his research was "sometimes."[1]

True morality comes from a heart turned inside out by what the Bible calls grace. The apostle Paul said: "Be transformed by the renewing of your mind, so that you may prove what the will of God is, that which is good and acceptable and perfect" (Romans 12:2). To "prove what the will of God is" means more than being able to give the right answer on moral issues. It involves more than just having information. We cannot claim to "prove" something and remain indifferent to it. Rather we must make it a part of our lives. And this is possible only as we find ourselves transformed by a renewing of our minds.

This radical change, which is the basis for right living, is not a natural process. Although both have their place, neither behavioral conditioning nor moral reasoning can accomplish it. The psalmist understood this when he wrote: "Create in me a clean heart, O God, and renew a right spirit within me" (Psalm 51:10, KJV). Heart renewal that results in true morality is an act of creation, and it is a gift from God.[2]

This is why the first commandment, which orders us to put away false gods, does not stop there. The text continues: "You shall have no other gods *before Me.*" The "other gods," who are actually no gods at all, are not to be replaced by a vacuum. After telling us what we are *not* to do (that is, not to worship false gods), the commandment then explains what we *are* to do. The prohibition then becomes a positive command to worship the true God.

Love and Worship

Once someone asked Jesus what the greatest commandment was. He replied by quoting Deuteronomy 6:5: "You shall love the Lord your God with all your heart, and with all your soul, and with all your mind." Then He added: "This is the great and first commandment" (Matthew 22:37, 38, RSV).

When Satan had attempted to tempt Him, Jesus

had said that the first commandment orders us to worship God. Here He says that it means we are to love Him.

"I love Danny. I just adore him," Jacqueline had declared. She wasn't thinking of biblical worship or adoration, of course, but she was closer to the truth than you might think, because worship, in the Bible, is an expression of love.

Worship, like love, is an attitude of the heart. It is a disposition and a decision to make God first, to put Him on life's throne and give Him His place as sovereign, making Him the ruler of our lives.

To give God His place as sovereign means that we will not attempt to subject Him to our preconceived ideas of what He is like or how He should do things. And we will reject the concept that we can believe in Him only insofar as we can understand Him. If we were to do this, then the starting point of faith would be atheism, and we could advance toward faith only by rational efforts. Furthermore, God would be limited by the size of our intellectual capacity. Then what we would be worshipping would no longer be God, but something finite, because we would know His length, breadth, and height, and His beginning and His end.[3]

This is not to say that the Christian faith has no place for reason and does not recognize the value of the evidence supporting it. There is nothing wrong with examining these evidences, but they are not its basis.

The knowledge of God begins not with human reason but with revelation. That is, God has to first reveal Himself. We cannot find out about Him through our own unaided efforts. And this revelation of God had its maximum expression in Jesus Christ. "No one has seen God at any time," the evangelist declared. "The only begotten son, who is in the bosom of the

Father, He has declared Him" (John 1:18, NKJV). From even His earliest years Jesus was engaged in teaching what God is like. When He gathered children in His arms and blessed them; when He taught His disciples along the lakeshore; when He calmed the storm and cleansed the Temple—in all these things He was saying: *God is like this. What I am and do, so is God.*

Just before Jesus was crucified, Philip said: "Lord, show us the Father" (John 14:8).

Jesus' reply has real pain in it: "Have I been so long with you, and yet you have not come to know Me, Philip? He who has seen Me has seen the Father; how can you say, 'Show us the Father'?" (verse 9).

Again and again the Gospels reveal Philip as a disciple slow to listen and quick to doubt. Unfortunately, I can empathize with that. But by having this attitude, Philip faced the serious danger of missing out, because the revelation of God never gets pounded into our brains by some overwhelming force. It goes quietly to those willing to open their eyes, ears, and, above all, their hearts. Instead of a monumental conviction, all we need is just a willingness to take down the roadblocks to faith, to stop shutting out the evidence.

As we accept the first commandment and grant God His place as true deity, that revelation will be imparted to us personally. And this is the only way anyone can receive it.

Making God first means to lay aside any idea, interest, or thought that competes with Him or diminishes His sovereignty in our life. This concept is the basis, the underlying principle, of true morality and spiritual living. It is an overarching principle that will allow us to evaluate the endless decisions and alternatives that face us day by day. In every case we will ask:

How will this video, this game, this friendship, this job, this possession, affect my relationship with God? When we actually begin to live this way, then order and morality will come creeping into our lives, peace will take the place of anguish, and hope will drive away depression and despair. Then and only then will we begin to understand the deeply spiritual kind of obedience that Jesus described in the Sermon on the Mount.

Why Is This Commandment First?

Even many people who instinctively believe in the existence of God don't reach the point of making Him number one in their lives. But that is really the only place He can occupy if He is, in fact, God. That is why this commandment comes first. All the others are simply moral rules that have no more power than thousands of other good ideas if we have not given God His place, if we have not made Him Sovereign and Lord of our lives.

The question is not: Do I already have a full and complete understanding about God and His will for my life? Neither is it: Am I good enough for Him to accept me? Am I already obeying the other commandments? You cannot back into the first commandment by obeying the other nine. Instead you have to come to the other nine through this one.

The question I need to ask myself is extremely simple but all-important: Am I willing to give Him His true and rightful place? Am I willing to make Him number one? That is what the first commandment is all about.

Here is an ancient appeal that still speaks to us across the centuries: "What does the Lord your God require from you, but to fear the Lord your God, to walk in all His ways and love Him, and to serve the

Lord your God with all your heart and with all your soul" (Deuteronomy 10:12).

---

[1] W. C. Crain, *Theories of Development* (New York: Prentice-Hall, 1985), pp. 118-136: "Kohlberg's scale has to do with moral thinking, not moral action. As everyone knows, people who can talk at a high moral level may not behave accordingly. Consequently, we would not expect perfect correlations between moral judgment and moral action. Still, Kohlberg thinks that there should be some relationship." See also Lawrence Kohlberg and Elliott Turiel, in C. S. Lesser, ed., *Psychology and Educational Practice* (Glenview, Ill.: Scott, Foresman, and Co., 1971), p. 458.

[2] "Anyone who is joined to Christ is a new being" (2 Corinthians 5:17, TEV).

[3] See Robert Wilkens, in *First Things* 37 (November 1993): 13-18.

LITTLE GODS

The Second Commandment

*You shall not make for yourself an idol, or any likeness
of what is in heaven above or on the earth beneath or
in the water under the earth. You shall not worship
them or serve them; for I, the Lord your God, am a
jealous God, visiting the iniquity of the fathers on the
children, on the third and the fourth generations of
those who hate Me, but showing lovingkindness to thousands,
to those who love Me and keep My commandments.*
—*Exodus 20:4-6*

It was early morning and still dark as we left home
and made our way through the deserted streets.
Soon the glow of the city had vanished behind us, and
we continued boring along the tunnel of light created
by our headlights. For a long time the only sound was
the hum of the engine and the tires on the pavement.

At last a touch of red on the horizon began to announce the approach of day, and before long we saw
it: a slim nail paring of intense luminosity. It was the
sun peeking from behind the nearby hill. Somehow,
without seeming to move, it slipped farther and farther into view until, a few minutes later, it was day.

It was our firstborn who broke the silence. Just 4
years old, David was constantly surprising us by his
curious observations.

"Daddy," he said, "if we come here early tomorrow morning and climb up that mountain, do you think we could reach out and touch the sun when it goes by?"

And I thought: *What an insight into a child's mind!* It's not that children consider them selves large—rather, that they make the world small. The vast immensities of the universe do not fit into their little minds, so they bring everything down to size.

Out there in the forest a man is working. "First I'll dig some clay," he says. "Then I'll shape it just so. See, here are the eyes and nose. Now I'll put it out in the sun for a while, and when it's dry I'll paint it with all my favorite colors. You want to know what I'm making? It's God, of course. Couldn't you tell? No, not God Himself. It's His portrait. This is what He looks like."

My 4-year-old thought that he could reach out with his little hand and touch the sun. And the man in the forest believes that he can make an image of God. Both are making the same mistake.

King Solomon had a better concept. He built a beautiful Temple in Jerusalem. When it was finished, he organized a celebration that lasted for days. But even in the midst of all the euphoria, he did not lose sight of the true meaning of the event. He spoke to God in prayer and said, "Behold, heaven and the heaven of heavens cannot contain thee; how much less this house which I have built!" (2 Chronicles 6:18, KJV).

Why does the second commandment forbid us to make an idol to represent God? Because no matter how big we make it, or how much gold, diamonds, or other things we use to cover it, the only thing it can do is make Him smaller. Inevitably we bring Him down to a strictly human concept of things. And that is really the heart of the problem. A poor mental image of God is the fundamental sin that the second commandment tries to help us avoid.

Modern rationalists commit the same error. They cast the little net of their intellectual skills into the vast ocean of the universe. What they can capture is limited by the brief radius of their senses and their ability to process the data they take in. They make themselves the owners of their bit of information and deny the existence of everything else. As I said, it is the same mistake, and proof that this problem is not limited to ignorant people.

"The Father Himself Loves You"

In ancient times the logical result of idolatry was polytheism, the belief that many gods exist. People invented more gods because they couldn't imagine that one was enough, that one deity could take care of everything.

The early Christians held fast to the idea that there was only one God, but many of them had a poor concept of who He was. They tended to think of Him as being like the deities they had once worshipped—beings who were forgetful and indifferent, not at all willing to help them. The converts from paganism felt that they had to beg and plead constantly to overcome His apathy and convince Him to take an interest in their needs.

It would be hard to imagine a greater error. The Bible compares God with the most powerful kind of human love, declaring: "Can a woman forget her nursing child and have no compassion on the son of her womb? Even these may forget, but I will not forget you. Behold, I have inscribed you on the palms of My hands" (Isaiah 49:15, 16).

But despite that assurance, many people still came to picture God as forgetful and reluctant, with an army of intercessors around His throne clamoring day and night for His attention to convince Him to help us. But Jesus told His followers: "I do not say to you that I will request of the Father on your behalf; for the

Father Himself loves you" (John 16:26, 27). And the apostle urged: "Let us draw near with confidence to the throne of grace, so that we may receive mercy and find grace to help in time of need" (Hebrews 4:16).

The idea of intercession by dead saints clearly violates the second commandment, because it is based on a pagan concept of a limited God who can hardly be convinced to help us.

"Why Did You Doubt?"

One day I was standing on the dock at Guanaja, Honduras, while a friend showed me the shrimp boats tied up to the dock there. They had their gantries raised, and the gigantic trawling nets dried in the sun. That evening they would go out again. The friend told me how many tons of shrimp the boats brought in every day.

Alarmed, I thought to myself, *At this rate, it won't be long before the oceans are depleted!*

The next morning I left, flying along the coast from Guanaja to Puerto Cabezas. Under the left wing of our plane we could see the blue outlines of the coastal mountains, and to the right, the immensity of the sea. I tried to guess how many miles away was the point where the horizon melted into the sky. We continued on our way, and a few minutes later I caught a glimpse of three shrimp boats far below us, bobbing and dipping in the waves as they dragged their nets behind them. They were some of the same ones I had seen the day before, but how tiny they appeared. And what a contrast between their size and the vastness of the ocean! Then I thought: *What can such tiny boats do to exhaust all the treasure that God has stored in His pantry?* How things change when we see them from a different perspective!

And I wondered, *What about God's perspective?* At times our problems seem to fill earth and sky. How do you think God views them?

That was the lesson Peter learned one stormy night on the Sea of Galilee. The gigantic waves and winds filled him with panic, and he shouted, "Lord, save me!" (Matthew 14:30).

"Immediately Jesus stretched out His hand and took hold of him, and said to him, 'You of little faith, why did you doubt?'" (verse 31).

Fear and anxiety come from a lack of faith, and they violate the second commandment, because they show that in our minds God is very small.

Never Underestimate the Power of an Idol

The psalmist wrote about idols: "Those who make them will become like them" (Psalm 115:8). The apostle Paul observed the same phenomenon in his day. He said that idolaters had exchanged "the glory of the incorruptible God for an image in the form of corruptible man and of birds and four-footed animals and crawling creatures.

"Therefore," he said, "God gave them over in the lusts of their hearts" "and to a depraved mind, to do those things which are not proper." He clarifies what he means by "not proper" with a list of sins that includes greed, evil, envy, murder, strife, deceit, malice, gossip, slander, insolence, arrogance, boasting, disobedience to parents, and being untrustworthy, unloving, and unmerciful (Romans 1:23, 28-31).

Not a very pretty picture, is it? But do you think it's an exaggeration? Recently I went to see the impressive ruins of Monte Albán in Oaxaca. It has images of the ancient Zapotec gods in the form of feathered serpents, crouching wild animals, and dozens of human figures. Violent expressions of anger and hatred distorted the faces of the idols. The guide showed us an altar where the priests ripped hearts from living victims on ceremonial occasions. Then he took us to a ball field, explaining that either the winning or the losing team was always slaughtered as a sacrifice to the gods.

"Those who make them will become like them," said the psalmist.

At noon I returned to the city and went into a local eatery. The place was vibrating to the ka-boom, ka-boom of a popular rhythm, and a modern "idol" was screaming:

> "All day long I dream about sex.
> And all night long I think about sex.
> And all the time I think about sex
> with you, with you."

The songs that followed were different only in that they used even more common street terms to re-peat the same message.

Who can doubt that modern idols have at least as much power over the people as the ancient ones? And it is still true that those who make them become like them. In many ways the results of modern idolatry are surpassing what the apostle Paul described in his day.

Thousands of Generations

Some people are surprised because the second com-mandment contains a serious warning about images: "You shall not worship them or serve them; for I, the Lord your God, am a jealous God, visiting the iniquity of the fathers on the children, on the third and the fourth generations of those who hate Me" (Exodus 20:5).

What startles them is that God says He is "jeal-ous." Furthermore, He declares that even the third and fourth generation are going to suffer because of the sins of their ancestors.

Their problem comes from a superficial reading of the text. Notice that what happens to "the third and fourth generation" is not a revenge taken on them by an angry God. The commandment says plainly that what is "visited" on them is the "iniquity of the fathers." This is exactly what the apostle Paul had in mind in the passage we cited earlier. He says that idol worship, the exaltation of the creature above the Creator, removes the barriers and opens the floodgates of human depravity. As people become like their idols, the earth becomes filled with violence, and people give their hearts over to "wickedness, greed, . . . envy, murder, strife, deceit, malice" (Romans 1:29). They become "slanderers, haters of God, insolent, arrogant, boastful, inventors of evil, disobedient to parents, without understanding, untrustworthy, unloving, unmerciful" (verses 30, 31). Do you think it would be a punishment to live in a society such as the one Paul portrays? This is the consequence that reaches to "the third and fourth generation," the fateful result that God wants us to avoid by giving us this warning in the second commandment. And this is why He is "jealous." Human jealousy is a display of self-interest, but the commandment makes it clear that God is jealous for His people.

By contrast, the mercy and "lovingkindness" of God will be on "thousands" of those who love Him and keep His commandments (Exodus 20:6). This refers, of course, to the promise of eternal life. Jesus said: "Father, I will that they also, whom thou hast given me, be with me where I am; that they may behold my glory, which thou hast given me: for thou lovest me before the foundation of the world" (John 17:24, KJV).

A Message of Freedom

The second commandment is the perfect complement of the first. People who have made a decision to put God at the center of their existence will not allow any created thing to occupy the place that belongs only to the Creator. And there will be no confusion with regard to the true worship, because they will turn away from anything that diminishes the importance of God in their lives.

For those to keep the first commandment and the second, obedience to the rest will be completely natural. If we love God—if He is on the throne of our lives—our hearts will overflow with love for other people as well.

The apostle James called the Ten Commandments "the perfect law, the law of liberty" (James 1:25). At this point we have looked at only two of its precepts, but the meaning of such perfection and freedom is already clear. As the psalmist says: "Great peace have they which love thy law: and nothing shall offend them" (Psalm 119:165, KJV).

A NAME TO HONOR

The Third Commandment

Thou shalt not take the name of the Lord thy God in vain, for the Lord will not hold him guiltless that taketh his name in vain.

—*Exodus 20:7, KJV*

It would be impossible to forget that united and enthusiastic family that my wife and I knew when we lived in Puerto Barrios, Guatemala. When we visited them in their home, they, with the courtesy so characteristic of Guatemalans, stood up one by one and introduced themselves. The first one to do so was the mother, Carmen Reyes. She explained that her husband was not present, because he no longer lived with the family. "When we began to study the Word of God, he became very angry and left," she told us sadly.

Then the others took their turn. "Isabel Reyes, your humble servant," the oldest said.

"Ramón Díaz," her brother, a good-looking lad of 17, introduced himself.

"María Reyes," the next one timidly said.

And so, with wide smiles and jokes between them, they continued until all of them had identified themselves.

We were curious why some of them went by Reyes and others by Díaz. But although we hesitated to ask, they soon made the reason clear. "Our dad," they said, "likes to drink, and every time one of us was born, he considered it another chance to celebrate. In this condition he would go down to the civil register to record our birth, and when the clerk would ask, 'Who is the father of this child?' sometimes he would give his name, but other times he would say, 'Who knows? I have no idea who the father is.' He thought this was funny, but the result is that some of us are officially recognized as his children and have his last name, whereas others are not, so we have to go by Mother's maiden name."

That family had accepted the situation, and we, of course, made no further comments, but we left there thinking: *How sad! How would it feel to know that your own father didn't recognize you, that he had not been willing to give you his family name.*

Jesus told the story of a boy who rebelled against his father and ran away from home. At last, after tremendous suffering, he came to his senses and turned his face toward home. Here is where we find one of the most beautiful verses in all of the Bible. It says: "While he was still a long way off, his father saw him and felt compassion for him, and ran and embraced him and kissed him" (Luke 15:20). Christ was trying to show us God's attitude toward all those who come to Him.

Jesus Himself said: "The one who comes to me I will certainly not cast out" (John 6:37). That takes us all in. Maybe we are coming with hesitation, half-doubting, half-believing, hardly understanding and still wondering if hope is possible. None of that matters. The key word is "Come!" Whoever comes will be "accepted in the beloved" (Ephesians 1:6, KJV). None will ever hear the words "I don't know whose child this is." In Christ we are all recognized; we are all legitimate sons and daughters.

"Do not fear," He says, "for I have redeemed you; I have called you by name; you are Mine!" (Isaiah 43:1). A beautiful assurance! But there is more. "When you pass through the waters, I will be with you; and through the rivers, they will not overflow you. When you walk through the fire, you will not be scorched, nor will the flame burn you" (verse 2). And these blessings are for "everyone who is called by My name" (verse 7).

Notice that it does not say that God's children will never have tough times. They may "pass through the waters," maybe even "through the fire." But the promise is sure: "The rivers . . . will not overflow you" and "the fire" will not "burn you." In the bitter hour "I will be with you." Why? Because you are "called by My name." "You are mine."

What a glorious privilege to bear the Father's name! In the face of this thought, the apostle Paul falls on his knees, exclaiming: "For this reason I bow my knees before the Father, from whom every family in heaven and on earth derives its name" (Ephesians 3:15). And the apostle John exclaims: "See how great a love the Father has bestowed upon us, that we would be called children of God" (1 John 3:1).

How Can We Be Sure That We Bear His Name?

Perhaps you find yourself wondering, *How can I bear this name? How can I be sure of being a member of the family of God both on earth and in heaven?* If so, congratulations! Of all the questions that one could ask in life, this is the most important.

The Lord Jesus Christ gave us the answer in the instruction that He provided His disciples. He told them: "Go therefore and make disciples of all the nations, baptizing them in the name of the Father and the Son and the Holy Spirit" (Matthew 28:19). It is through baptism that we come to take on us this holy name.

What thoughsts come to your mind when you hear the word "baptism"?

"Well," one young man said to me once, "when I hear this word, I remember the baptism of my infant niece. Her parents held the baby in their arms. All of us relatives and friends stood with them and the god-parents in a circle around the baptismal font. We all listened while the priest touched her forehead with water and pronounced the solemn words: *'Ego baptizo te in nomine Patris, et Filii, et Spiritus Sancti. Amén.'*

"Then we all said reverently 'Aaaaaa-men!' "

The Latin word *baptizo* pronounced by the priest on that occasion comes from an identical Greek term. In the first century the common people used it to refer to the act of placing something in the water. When John the Baptist—literally, "the baptizer"—began to baptize people in the Jordan (John 3:23), the rite was not new, because the Jews had purification rites in which they immersed themselves in tanks of water to wash away their impurities.

The apostle Paul also related Christian baptism to these Jewish rites, calling it the "washing of re-generation" (Titus 3:5). But in his letter to the Romans he added a new dimension to the symbol-ism that greatly enriches it: "We have been buried with [Christ] through baptism," he wrote (Romans 6:4). In another place Paul clarified what he meant by saying: "I have been crucified with Christ" (Galatians 2:20).

The change that takes place when we turn our lives over to Christ is so great that it is no exaggeration to speak of it as a "death" or even "crucifixion." It is the execution of the sinful person we used to be. When we are transformed by the renewing of our un-

derstanding (Romans 12:2), the old disorderly and destructive thought patterns disappear. New tastes and
new values take over. Our motives and goals are so
different that it can truly be said that the individual we
were before has died and a new one has been born.
Water baptism is the burial of that dead person.

At the same time it is a celebration of the new
birth. It is a birth announcement, a visible testimony of
something that is invisible, although it is very real. And
it is a way of publicly announcing that new and very
different person who now resides in the old house.

Children Look Like Their Parents

When a baby is born, people like to look for sim-
ilarities:

"He has his mother's nose," says one.

"He resembles my aunt Janie," the mother declares.

"No," says the father proudly, "I think he looks
like me."

If we are really God's children through the new
birth, we will be like our heavenly Father. When
people be able to can say about us "He is kind and patient" or "She is humble and helpful," then they can
also add: "This really is a son or daughter of God."

Jesus said: "Love your enemies . . . that you may
be sons of your Father who is in heaven" (Matthew
5:44, 45). How does the act of being kind to those
who don't deserve it show that we are God's children? Because that's how God is. "He causes His sun
to rise on the evil and the good, and sends rain on the
righteous and the unrighteous" (verse 45).

This helps us understand the meaning of the third
command when it says that we must not take God's
name in vain.

Taking the name of God in vain is to call ourselves a son or daughter of God and yet continue with the same life as before. It means to assume that sacred name without experiencing any real change in who we are. As a result, it amounts to adopting the name of a family without really belonging to it.

How Much Is a Name Worth?

Teri Hatcher valued her name at a very high price when she sued the London *Daily Sport*. The paper had published an article stating that the actress left her 7-year-old daughter locked up at home while she went out with a series of lovers. The court agreed that the periodical had defamed her name, and its publisher had to pay a high price for the damage the article had done.

How much would you say God's name is worth? When we do not live up to our Christian commit-ment, we are making Him look bad. We are dragging the family name through the mud. The apostle Paul spoke of some people who were doing it in his day, declaring that "the name of God is blasphemed among the Gentiles because of you" (Romans 2:24).

We also make Him look bad when we use the sa-cred name in a light or trifling way or employ it as a vul-garity or obscenity. When we do that, we tell everyone that God's name is not sacred, that it has no value or im-portance to us. It would be even more serious to use God's name to affirm something that is false, or to fail to fulfill a promise that we have made in His name.

A Promise Kept

In the first chapter I made a promise. I said that I would never ask you to accept blindly any of the ideas in this book, but that you would have plenty of op-portunity to test their validity. How can you do the testing in this case?

If it were an issue of a subjective philosophy, it would be a matter of expressing various opinions and discussing them. In the case of simple subjective reflections and curious proposals, we could turn them around in our minds, looking at them from side to side, as we meditate or speculate about them. But this is not the case.

Here we are talking about "commandments," each of them expressed in imperative terms. It does not say: "It seems to me that it might be preferable if you didn't have other gods." Or "you really ought to consider the possibility of discarding the worship of images." What they demand of us is obedience.

This means that the testing of statements is through application, not analysis. Precisely for this reason, the proof of their validity will come in the way of the marvelous results, the fruits, that will appear in the life of those who put them into practice.

The first commandment encourages us to love God and place Him in the center of our existence, and the second clarifies further what that means. Now the third commandment takes into account the first two and says to us: *What are you going to do about this? Will you accept the invitation that your heavenly Father has given you? Are you going to place Him in the center of your existence, and bear His name and His character?*

Our answer will determine whether He is able to pour out on our life the abundant blessings that He has promised in His Word.

FINDING PEACE

The Fourth Commandment

Remember the sabbath day, to keep it holy. Six days you shall labor and do all your work, but the seventh day is a sabbath of the Lord your God; in it you shall not do any work, you or your son or your daughter, your male or your female servant or your cattle or your sojourner who stays with you. For in six days the Lord made the heavens and the earth, the sea and all that is in them, and rested on the seventh day; therefore the Lord blessed the sabbath day and made it holy.

—*Exodus 20:8-11*

I have no idea how many times I traveled by passenger launch to the port of Livingston on the northeastern coast of Guatemala, but it was a lot. Nevertheless, one such trip was like no other.

It was only about 5:00 p.m. when we pulled away from the dock in Puerto Barrios, but it was already starting to get dark. An insistent rain was falling, so instead of enjoying the breezes on the deck, everyone jammed into the little cabin. As soon as we moved out from behind the seawall the storm struck us with its full fury.

Violent gusts of wind lashed the rain against the windows with an intensity that threatened to break them. With one hand I clung to the forward bulkhead to keep from falling and with the other held my head, longing for a way to calm the overwhelming nausea that only grew worse with each heave and pitch. Conversation was impossible, but I could hear moans and, at times, prayers or curses from the other passengers. On previous trips distant points of light that winked at us from houses along the shore had marked our progress. Now we could hardly make out the bow of the ship.

The voyage usually took about 90 minutes, but this time it seemed eternal. In fact, I was beginning to think that the captain must have lost his way and that we were heading out to open sea, when suddenly the most incredible calm overtook us. Instead of tossing and pitching, the little ship began gliding steadily across the water, and, up ahead, we could see through the rain the cheerful lights of our destination.

What had made the difference? The storm was not over, but we had entered the shelter of the harbor. Out in the open ocean the waves still raged as wildly as ever, but they could no longer terrify us, because we had come into the refuge, and we were safe.

The Bible says that in the beginning the whole earth was involved in a storm that was incomparably worse that the one we experienced that night. Wrapped in impenetrable darkness, water, air, rocks and earth churned about in a chaotic maelstrom (Genesis 1:1, 2).[1]

Then God spoke, and the darkness gave way to light. He spoke again, and the atmosphere sprang into existence, continents appeared, mountains rose up, and the sea was contained in its bed. What these details are telling us is that the process of creation was a movement from disorder to order, from turbulence to calm.

It is interesting to note that God recorded His satisfaction with what was taking place. Verse 10 says: "God saw that it was good." Why would He have said this for the first time precisely at this point on the third day? Maybe it was because light, air, water, and earth now existed. They were the four elements needed to sustain plant life. In other words, they made everything ready for the next step.

Later on that same day, the earth put on a green dress. Grasses, broadleafs, mosses, and ferns appeared. Majestic trees raised their arms toward heaven. Pines and flowers added color to the landscape and per-fumed the air.

Vegetation, with its marvelous process of photo-synthesis, was designed to serve animal life, producing food and oxygen. And for the second time on the same day, God spoke and said that "it was good" (verse 12).

On the fifth day and early on the sixth, God spoke again, and the sea and earth and skies teemed with creatures that swam, flew, walked, or crawled. Once again the Creator expressed His satisfaction with the results (verse 25).

"Then God said, 'Let Us make man in Our image, according to Our likeness; and let them rule over the fish of the sea and over the birds of the sky and over the cattle and over all the earth, and over every creep-ing thing that creeps on the earth" (verse 26).

The creation of intelligent beings to govern the earth was the last step in God's conquest of chaos by order. Then, with infinite joy, the Creator contem-plated His finished work, and this time He did not simply say it was good. He announced that "it was *very good"* (verse 31).

Science assures us that matter consists of electrons and protons that are actually a form of energy, but en-ergy that is tightly ordered. Matter is categorized in the form of elements that start with hydrogen, the lightest and simplest of them all, and go on finally to heavy elements that are radioactive and so unstable that they exist for only a fraction of a second.

The elements bond together, forming molecules that in turn range from simple ones, such as table salt, to extremely complex ones that occur only in living organisms and therefore are called organic molecules. A single molecule of protein may have tens of millions of atoms. And every living organism, from the tiniest microbe to the largest whale, consists of them.

So, even on the level of elements and molecules, Creation was a march toward order and organization. Every step forward in this process implied thousands, and in some cases billions, of changes.

Contrary to Nature

Physicists have synthesized three laws of thermo–dynamics. The second law states that all systems in nature show an invariable trend and movement toward disintegration, disorder, and loss of energy. Scientists call it the principle of entropy.

Creation involved precisely the opposite. Through biochemical and physical transformations of immense complexity, God turned a chaotic planet into a world of order. When He said that it was "very good," it was because the storm was over, disorder had been conquered, chaos was gone, and the whole earth was a peaceful symbiosis in all of its different parts and relationships. Each element and every detail of Creation was designed to serve others. With one voice, everything testified to the love and infinite wisdom of the One who had designed and brought it all into existence.

There is no coincidence in the relationship of ideas found in God's final pronouncement at the end of the Creation account. It tells us that:

(a) God saw that it was very good, and then

(b) He rested.

It is clear that the Creator's rest has nothing to do with fatigue. It is rest that comes when order takes the place of chaos—the peace and the calm that follow the storm. God saw that the earth was at rest, and then He rested.

The Work Is Finished

Here is the passage in which God's declaration appears. Notice especially the terms I have numbered:

"God saw all that He had *made* (1), and behold, it was very good. And there was evening and there was morning, the sixth day. Thus the heavens and the earth were *completed* (2), and all their hosts. By the seventh day God *completed* (3) His work which He had *done* (4), and He rested on the seventh day from all His work which He had *done* (5). Then God blessed the seventh day and sanctified it, because in it He rested from all His work which God had *created* (6) and *made* (7)" (Genesis 1:31-2:3).

Seven times this brief passage reminds us that Creation was a finished work. This means that God "rested"—that is, He ceased and stopped what He was doing, because He had completed His divine task. *The point is that there was no oversight—nothing was omitted or overlooked.* No part did not function in perfect harmony with all the others. "God saw all that He had made, and behold, it was very good."

Sign of a Perfect Provision

An illustration can serve to clarify the importance of this point. Try to imagine for a moment that Adam, when first created, might have sprung to his feet and said, "Lord, don't You need me to help You with something?"

At this the Creator would have smiled and replied, "No, Adam; the work is done."

"But there must be something I can do. Maybe I could paint some decorations on the butterfly's wings."

"No, the butterfly's wings already have their colors."

"H'mm, well . . . maybe I could teach the birds to sing."

"No, they already know how to sing much better than you could ever teach them."

"What if I would check the air to see if it has the right amount of oxygen? You know that a little too much or not enough is dangerous. Maybe I could help You calibrate it."

"No, I already took care of that, too."

"But Lord, there must something I can do."

"Yes, in fact, there is."

"What is it, Lord?"

"I want you to rest."

"Rest! But how can I rest when I haven't done any work?"

"I want you to trust Me, Adam. You need to believe that, in fact, the work is done, that I really have made a complete and perfect provision for all your needs."

And that is the meaning of the rest on the seventh day. If the Creator had brought human beings to life at the beginning of the week and had asked us to help out in some way, or at least had requested our opinion, we could take some credit, couldn't we? But He didn't. The observance of the Sabbath was from the beginning, is now, and always will be a celebration of God's work and not ours. Like Adam, we rest to show that we accept this reality, that we trust in God's perfect provision for our well-being and fulfillment. It means that we repose confidently in His hands, trusting in His wisdom, His plan and provision for our lives.

In conclusion, we concede to God His position as

Creator and accept ours as creatures. Thus, in a deep and meaningful sense, our rest on the seventh day is an act of worship.

In nearly every false religion, including false Christianity, worship is a matter of *doing*. Only in the Bible are we instructed to worship by leaving off our own doing, laying aside our effort and struggles, to cease our labor and *rest* in the serene confidence that the *work* on our behalf is all done. The fourth commandment declares: "The seventh day is a sabbath." The word "sabbath" itself means, literally, "rest." The seventh day is the rest appointed by God Himself. It is the day in which He invites us to join Him in His rest—"in it you shall not do any work."

By resting with Him, we declare to the universe that the Sabbath rest is a sign of a relationship with God based on faith.[2]

But our rest on the Sabbath not only symbolizes this relationship—it promotes and deepens it, becoming a part of its reality. Our rest on the seventh day not only declares that we find assurance, and therefore peace, in God's love; it strengthens this assurance. It affirms, and at the same time confirms, the relationship between God and His creation.

That is why the Sabbath is the complement and guarantee of the first three commandments, which order us to worship God and give Him first place in our lives.

It might be possible to keep the first three commandments in our hearts, to observe them in some way that would not be immediately evident to other people. We could decide in our hearts to honor God and make Him first. It is quite possible that no one would notice that we did not bow down to images. But this wouldn't be true with regard to Sabbath observance. Immediately obvious, it is a public announcement. This may be the reason that Scripture says that the Sabbath is a "sign" of the covenant between God and His people (Ezekiel 20:12, 20).

A Commandment of Mercy

Do you have any idea how many people feel desperate and frustrated with the responsibilities and problems of life? We hurry and worry, but there is never "enough time." All of us feel burdened with the need to make a living, keep up our home, improve our relationships, educate our children, care for our health, get a degree, pay bills, and pursue a career. These and thousands of other tasks constantly clamor for our attention. The problem is that we are finite, and life never stops demanding more and more. When the famous empire builder Cecil Rhodes lay dying, he supposedly muttered, "So little done—so much to do." Countless people today echo his frustration.

In the midst of the onrushing fury of events and the strident demands of a life that, like the mouth of the grave, never cries "Enough!" the great Creator-God offers us the Sabbath. Author Herman Wouk, who observed the Sabbath, wrote: "The Sabbath is the arms of a mother that reach out to receive a weary child."

"Six days you are to labor," says the commandment. This is your allotted time. Work, struggle, and give it your best during it. But all this has a limit—the Sabbath. In it you are to rest.

The fourth commandment commands us to work, but it does not say: "Work until you fall exhausted." Neither does it tell us to keep toiling until the work is done—that you can rest only when you finish. Rather it declares that you are to work, yes, but there is a limit to what you have to do.

The Sabbath is a parable of life because it teaches us that we will come to the end of our days and draw our last breath still thinking of more we would like to do—if we only had the time. It teaches us to do what we can in our allotted time, and then rest. From it we learn to measure our achievement not by the standard of our own perfection but by that of God's love.

The one who made us knows that our selfish ambition, and at times even our sincere desire to do our best, can lead us to intemperance and excess. Therefore, He has given us the fourth precept of the Decalogue as a commandment of mercy. "Six days you are to labor," He says, "but on the seventh you will rest."

Jesus reminded the people in His day that the Sabbath was made *for* humanity (Mark 2:27). It is a precious gift provided for our benefit and protection. The Sabbath is a harbor, our shelter from the interminable storm of existence, an oasis where the weary traveler can find restoration and renewal before again taking up the struggles of life.

The Sabbath in a Broken World

"Did God really say you are not to eat the fruit from any tree of the garden?"

It must have seemed like an innocent question.

And the woman, unsuspecting, was quick to answer. She would defend the Creator from a false accusation. "Not true!" she said. "We are allowed to eat the fruit from the trees of the garden. But regarding the fruit of the tree in the middle of the garden, God has said, 'You shall not eat of it or touch it, lest you die.'"

"Of course you won't die!" the enemy smirked. "It's just that God knows that when you eat from it your eyes will be opened, and you will be like Him, knowing good and evil" (see Genesis 3:1-5). *Here is something that God doesn't want you to know. He is with-holding information that would be for your benefit.*

The Sabbath was a message of faith: "Trust Me. Accept that I really have made a perfect provision." But the enemy's message is precisely the opposite: "It is not true that God has made a perfect provision. Something is lacking. You need to separate yourselves from His plan, choose your own way, and fend for yourselves."

By accepting his insinuations, Adam and Eve joined the enemy in his attitude of distrust and in his disobedience. This brought in the need for an additional provision, a plan by which God could rescue human beings from their confusion and restore them to a relationship of faith, trust, and obedience.

It was on a Friday when God concluded His work and rested from the finished task of Creation. And it was also on a Friday when the Jesus finished the work of redemption. And as He bowed his head and died, he said, "It is finished!" (John 19:30).

After that, the disciples had just enough time to remove His body from the cross and lay it in Joseph's new tomb. As they hastened away, the sun was setting, and Scripture says, "The Sabbath was about to begin" (Luke 23:54). Then, for the second time, the Savior rested on the seventh day from a finished work.

The Sabbath, created to commemorate God's provision for a perfect world, then took on an additional meaning. From that day forward it would also symbolize His provision for a world in sin—His plan to redeem and heal and restore us to a relationship of faith and trust in Him.

This second meaning of the Sabbath was anticipated long before the cross. When the Lord gave the Ten Commandments at Sinai, He explained the reason for the Sabbath by pointing back to Creation. But when Moses repeated them 40 years later, He quoted them in a way that clearly foreshadowed the second reason: "Remember that you were a slave in the land of Egypt, and the Lord your God brought you out from there by a mighty hand and by an outstretched arm; *therefore* the Lord your God commanded you to observe the sabbath day" (Deuteronomy 5:15).

God created human beings to occupy a position of rulership (Genesis 1:26, 27). Slavery is the opposite of this. Not only had the Lord rescued His people from literal slavery, but it was His intention to restore them to their trust relationship with Him (Exodus 19:4), and as a result to a leadership position by elevating them to a "royal priesthood" (see verses 5, 6; 1 Peter 2:9; Revelation 5:10).

Thus the Sabbath is a celebration not only of Creation but of also of redemption.

We have noticed already the meaning of the Sabbath as a complement and guarantee of the first three commandments. But as a sign of our redemption from slavery, the Sabbath also brings home to our conscience the need to respect our fellow humans. It tells us to remember the quarry from which we were dug (Isaiah 51:1). Thus the fourth commandment also gives meaning to the following six precepts, which deal with our duty toward other people (see also Deuteronomy 16:11, 12).

Entering Into His Rest

Many times it seems as if the second law of thermodynamics is trying to impose itself in my life, and that the principle of disorder is going to win. I have even thought that the experience of that stormy night on the journey to Livingston was destined to be a permanent reality in my existence.

I suspect the apostle Paul might have felt something like this when he confessed: "I am not practicing what I would like to do, but I am doing the very thing I hate. . . . The good that I want, I do not do, but I practice the very evil that I do not want. . . . For I joyfully concur with the law of God in the inner man, but I see a different law in the members of my body, waging war against the law of my mind and making me a prisoner of the law of sin which is in my members" (Romans 7:15-23).

With total honesty the great apostle admits that he is a perfectly normal human being and that spiritual storms are a reality in his life just as they are for the rest of us. It is an experience that every human being convinced of a need for change and improvement, yet finding themselves locked in mortal combat with old habits and passions, can understand and appreciate.

Are we condemned always to flounder in the midst of a relentless storm? No, in the same passage the apostle tells us where to find the harbor: "Thanks be to God," he exclaims (verse 25). "There is now no condemnation for those who are in Christ Jesus. For the law of the Spirit of life in Christ Jesus has set you free from the law of sin and of death" (Romans 8:1, 2).

In another place Scripture speaks of the Sabbath as a type or symbol of this spiritual rest that God grants His children. "There remains a Sabbath rest for the people of God. For the one who has entered His [God's] rest has himself also rested from his works, as God did from His" (Hebrews 4:9, 10).

Adam accepted that God really had made a perfect provision in His finished work of creation, and he showed this acceptance by resting on the Sabbath. Christians join him in celebrating the goodness and loving provision of God in the Creation. By withdrawing from the furious pace of our habitual activities, by stepping out from under the pressure of life during the Sabbath hours, we remind ourselves that the world doesn't revolve around us, that the sun doesn't rise in the morning and that flowers don't bloom at our command, and that creation can get along perfectly well without any help at all from us. Our physical rest on the Sabbath celebrates and acknowledges the marvelous provision for us in the physical world, just as it has for God's people since the world began.

And our faith in Jesus adds a glorious new dimension of richness to all of this. As the passage from Hebrews 4 points out, the Sabbath rest now means that we accept that Christ really has achieved our salvation on the cross of Calvary.

Because of this finished work, the Christian can "rest from his works," that is, from the frustrating and hopeless effort to earn salvation through personal good deeds. We can simply accept by faith that when Jesus said "It is finished," it really was, and that He had achieved a salvation full and unlimited for "whoever believes" (John 3:16).

This trust relationship with God and the experience of living faith that is symbolized and deepened when we rest on the seventh day is "the peace of God, which surpasses all comprehension" (Philippians 4:7). It is the rest that is enjoyed by all those who are "in Christ Jesus." They no longer need to be tossed to and fro in a sea of problems and anxieties. They can enter the port and find peace and rest.

Maybe you are wondering what to do about all this. I urge you to hesitate no longer. With joyful and confident steps, enter into the Sabbath rest. "Let us fear if, while a promise remains of entering His rest, any one of you should seem to have come short of it" (Hebrews 4:1).

---

[1] I make no apology for dealing with the early chapters of Genesis as serious history. But I do understand the misgivings of some who think differently. They believe that these Bible stories do not represent real events. They see them, rather, as didactic tools or teaching messages. In either case, it is clear that any approach to understanding the Ten Commandments will have to deal with these chapters, because they are foundational to comprehending the moral law and, in fact, to the entire message of the Bible.

[2] Ironic, isn't it, that some people accuse Sabbath observers of believing in salvation by works when, in fact, it means just the opposite?

PARENTS AND CHILDREN

The Fifth Commandment

Honor your father and your mother,
that your days may be prolonged
in the land which the Lord your God gives you.
                                    —*Exodus 20:12*

Eleni Gatzoyiannis lived in Greece when a civil war threatened to tear it apart (1946-1949), and when the Communists seized her house for their headquarters, she let them have it. When they put her to work on community improvement projects and conscripted her eldest daughter for the army, she did not refuse. She could still hope that all this was temporary and that one day things would be right again.

But then they announced they were taking her boys, 6 and 8 years old, to another country where they would be retrained in Communist Party principles. In her inmost being she knew it could not be, and she began to plan their escape. She realized that if she herself tried to take them through the rebel lines to the next village, where their uncle could help them, they would never make it, but she reasoned correctly that two children walking along the road together would not draw much attention. By the early light of dawn she went with them as far as she dared. Then with a last fervent embrace she hurried them on their way. The last thing the boys saw as they turned to look back was their mother still waving to them in the distance.

When the comrades came for the boys, she tried to put them off, but the truth soon came out. The rebel leaders imprisoned her in the basement of her own house and tortured her, then took her out to the orchard and stood her before a firing squad. Those who witnessed the scene said that just before the shots rang out, she raised her arms and cried out, "My children! My children!"

One can understand why the story of this brave mother has stirred the hearts of millions. It touches a cord in every heart, because the relationship between parents and children is universal in its scope. Eleni did what every mother feels that she would do if the circumstances required it. Most parents would die for their children, not with doubt or hesitation, but gladly.

The fifth commandment addresses this powerful relationship from the bottom up—it speaks to the children. And for good reason: not everyone marries, and many people never become parents, but everyone is a son or a daughter. Our relationship to our parents, or even the lack of it, affects every one of us for good or for evil to the last day of our lives. And this is precisely what the fifth commandment is all about. It is about an attitude and a relationship.

We cannot change the reality into which we were born. None of us had any voice in choosing our parents, and neither can we make them over according to our ideas of how they should be. One biblical writer recalled that our parents "disciplined us for a short time as seemed best to them" (Hebrews 12:10). They may have done their job with consummate skill; they may have done it with many mistakes and blunders; or—like most of us—with some of both. What they did or did not do inevitably had an impact on us; but it can never be said too loudly or repeated too often: we are affected more deeply and permanently by our attitude toward their efforts than by the specific method they used. And this is precisely what the fifth commandment addresses. It lays the burden for the success of the relationship between parents and children at the place where the buck really does stop. The commandment focuses on the aspect of the relationship that influences us first and most, and it is the one about which we do have a choice. Although we can neither choose our parents nor change them, the attitude we have toward them is definitely up to us.

For many years I sat on the discipline committee of a Christian university. One day a student who was practically a case study in body language sat across the table from us. Our committee was less interested in discovering specific details of what he had done than in his attitude toward continuing in the university, and the answer seemed clear enough. He glared at us fiercely, his arms folded over his chest. The interview that followed was not surprising. Everything we said and every question we asked him brought an angry outburst or a retort. Before long the committee members began shaking their heads and glancing at one another.

After a few minutes in which we were obviously getting nowhere, I said, "Paul, I want to understand what it is you are trying to tell us. Even the simplest question we ask you gets an angry reply. What's the matter? What are you trying to say?"

He didn't answer, but turned his glare directly on me. I saw his jaws clench and unclench. After another pause I continued: "I wonder if maybe you see yourself in an adversarial relationship with us, as if you and the committee are on the opposite sides, and we are at war with each other. Is that how you feel?"

With this his defiant glare seemed to soften a bit,

but still he remained silent until I said, "How is it with you and your dad, Paul? Are you like this with him, too? Is that what you're bringing here today?"

Then, for the first time, he looked down, and the expression on his face turned almost wistful. Finally he said softly, "Yes, that's how it is."

Was Paul out to hurt and embarrass his father? I think maybe he was. It was certainly in his power to do so. In this life we find ourselves judged by the results we achieve more than by what we did or didn't do to reach them. Nowhere is this more true than in parenting. And it is also true that nobody can hurt us as much as someone we love.

But it didn't take much effort to figure out that the person affected most by Paul's attitude was the young man himself. His present and future were on the line because of his unresolved anger. Our efforts that day, and subsequent counseling, were unsuccessful, and soon after the interview he plunged over the cliff that he was so near to at that time.

As Paul's case so clearly illustrates, the way we feel about our parents—our attitude toward them, the deep gut-level reaction evoked in us when we think of them—will profoundly shape the way we relate to all authority and, to a lesser degree, to all other human beings. And in all likelihood it will affect our relationship with God as well.

The principle laid down in the fifth commandment is a strong foundation for success in school, on the job, and even in marriage. In fact, the first time the Bible mentions marriage it describes it as a man leaving his father and mother and joining himself to his wife (Genesis 2:24). So the Bible sees even marriage as a transference and, in some sense, a continuation of a relationship that started with our parents. People who have unresolved issues with their parents head into marriage with a serious handicap, and they are at extremely high risk for having problems in other areas of life as well. That is why the commandment says that if we honor our parents our life will be "prolonged in the land which the Lord your God gives you" (Exodus 20:12). This means that a healthy relationship with our parents is the basis for good relations, peace of mind, and success throughout our life span.

Honor Is an Attitude of the Heart

The Ten Commandments seem to divide into two groups. Four focus on our relationship to God, and the remaining six teach us how to interact with other human beings. The first commandment tells us to worship our heavenly Father. This one, the initial one in the human relations group, requires us to honor our parents.

Honor, like worship, is an attitude of the heart. It refers not to a specific action or behavior toward our parents, but rather to the way we choose to relate to them.

The apostle Paul tells us that the fifth commandment requires children to obey their parents (Ephesians 6:1). When some people, including some parents, hear the word "obedience," they immediately think of control. They interpret it in the way a machine acts when you open a valve or turn a switch. But the obedience that springs from an attitude of "honor" is an intelligent response, an active expression of love and respect, not an automated compliance with authority.

Notice how the wise man highlights this idea: "My son, observe the commandment of your father and do not forsake the teaching of your mother; bind them continually on your heart; tie them around your neck.

When you walk about, they will guide you; when you sleep, they will watch over you; and when you awake, they will talk to you" (Proverbs 6:20-22). Notice that he is describing an attitude. Obedience without the attitude of honor is heavy drudgery. In fact, it is slavery.

Honoring our parents means we will want to make them look good by being good ourselves, and to make them successful in their efforts to help us be successful. The fifth commandment tells us to pull off our boxing gloves and get out of the ring, listen to their counsel, speak well of them, and look for ways to show them our appreciation and respect. Again we hear from the wise man: "Let your father and your mother be glad, and let her rejoice who gave birth to you" (Proverbs 23.25).

The principle of honor does not vary, but the way it applies changes throughout life. It alters according to the time and circumstances. Shortly after graduating from college I had the privilege of enjoying the friendship of Henry Baasch. Born about 1885 in Hamburg, Germany, he was a man rich in experience, good humor, and wisdom.

One day he said to me, "Are you your father's son?"

"Uh, well, yes, I guess so," I replied, not sure what he meant.

"I suppose you are," he said. "You're only 21, aren't you? Don't worry; that will change. First your father is your father; then he becomes your son. It has already happened to me, you know. Now my son is my father. He tells me what to do, and I have to listen to him."

The principle of honor will express itself differently for a 5-year-old than for someone who is 14. And at 14 it is not the same as at 25. The advancing weakness and infirmity of our parents as they age brings further changes. Honoring them then takes on still another dimension. Failure to recognize and adapt to these changing circumstances by either side is a formula for problems. But when the relationship goes well, it is in the sunset of life that we can most fully appreciate the meaning of David's words:

> "Behold, children are a gift of the Lord;
> The fruit of the womb is a reward.
> Like arrows in the hand of a warrior,
> So are the children of one's youth.
> How blessed is the man whose quiver
> is full of them" (Psalm 127:3-5).

Of course, even the death of our parents does not cancel our obligation to honor them. What we do and how we live still can make them look good and honor their memory. We can live in a way that expresses gratitude for what they stood for and what we received from them.

Placing the Responsibility Where It Belongs

By addressing the offspring rather than the parents, the fifth commandment places the responsibility where it ultimately belongs.

For most of us it is true that our parents make a bigger difference in our lives than any other human being ever will. Whoever becomes a parent undertakes a great responsibility. But the commandment focuses our attention at the crucial point of the children's attitude to the relationship, because that is, ultimately, what will make the biggest difference. Our parents can discipline us, they can counsel us, they can set us a good example, they can cry over us and pray for us. But they can never do for us the one thing that makes all the difference. They cannot take away from us the power of decision. The greatest honor we can bring them is not by our words or by heaping flowers on their tombs, but by being the kind of people we ought to be. And the choice to do this rests entirely in our hands.

One of the happy results of having spent a lifetime in the classroom is that I have a lot of young friends who never fail to show enthusiastic goodwill to help out when they see a real need. Suppose I were to roll my car out of the driveway one of these mornings and wait till some of my young friends come along. Calling them over, I say, "I wonder if you could give me a push." Do you think they would turn me down? Of course they wouldn't.

Then when they've pushed me about a block and I see they are getting tired, I announce, "OK. I sure do appreciate it. That's far enough." Then, as soon as they are gone, I see if I can get somebody else to do the same.

It might be possible to repeat this strategy three or four times, but before long somebody will ask, "Where is it you are trying to get to? Do you want us to push you to the gas station or the repair shop?"

At that point I will have to tell them the truth. "Uh, not exactly. It's just that, well . . . I need to get to Monterey, and you know how the price of gas has been going up lately."

Do you think my plan would succeed?

Now, as I said, I know a lot of really great young people. They are good-hearted and always ready for a joke and for having fun, and when someone gives them a nudge in the right direction for their lives, they don't rebel or resist. They will head in the right direction for a while, but before long they coast to a stop and stand around joking some more and fooling away their time, waiting for someone to give them another shove.

Now, don't get me wrong—we all need some good counsel and a word of encouragement. A good spiritual shove at the right time may be just what it takes to get us started. Maybe at times this will even include some serious correction or rebuke, but sooner or later—and much better if it is sooner rather than later—we have to start our own engines. Nobody is going to push me all the way to Monterey, and nobody is going to push you into heaven, either.

See if you can imagine the following scene: A woman arrives at the gates of heaven and tries to slip in without being noticed. "Just a minute," the Gatekeeper says. "Where are you going?"

"Who, me?" She seems to be really nervous about something. "Uh, well, it's just that I read where it says that if I wash my robes and make them white in Jesus' blood, I can enter in through the gates into the city [Revelation 22:14]. So I that's what I did—I washed them, and here I am."

"But I notice that you are carrying something there under your robe. What is that?"

At this the poor woman looks more nervous than ever. It seems as though she is about to cry. "Oh, that. It's just something that . . . uh . . . something I wanted to bring in with me."

"What is it?"

Now her tears start to fall. "Lord, it's one of my children. I want so much for him to be here with me. Please, can't I bring him in too?"

Now, if you think this scene is only humorous, maybe you haven't realized yet how much parents long to give their children the most precious thing they could ever wish for them, and how much their joy and peace of mind are tied to this issue.

But it can never be. The prophet Ezekiel makes a

vivid comparison. He says that even if Noah, Daniel, and Job were alive today, by their faithfulness they could not save anyone but themselves (Ezekiel 14:20). And that's the way it is, because faith is not transferable.

We sometimes say that God has no grandchildren. It's also true that He has no nieces or nephews, no in-laws or anything else. He has nothing but children. What this means is that we cannot establish a relation-ship with God through someone else's faith or get to heaven by hanging on to their coattails. Our parents may have been good people. If so, we should be thankful—not everyone has that privilege. But we have to do something more than just admire them. We have to make our own decision and accept the sacrifice of Jesus on our behalf. Establishing our own personal relationship with God, we must ourselves enter the spiritual discipline of prayer and faith, and experience for ourselves "the washing of regeneration and renewing by the Holy Spirit" (Titus 3:5).

This is why the fifth commandment addresses the children rather than the parents, because there is where the buck really does stop.

The Other Side of Honor

Of course, nothing we have said before lessens or minimizes the responsibility of parents or justifies them in feeling they have little or no accountability for how they deal with their children. It is clearly im-possible to consider children's attitude toward their parents without also seeing it as a two-sided coin, be-cause the interaction between parents and children is profoundly reciprocal. When the apostle Paul speaks about the fifth commandment, he makes it clear that children's duty to honor their parents is matched by the parents' duty toward their children (Ephesians

6:1-4; Colossians 3:20, 21).

We have noticed that the honor that children are to give their parents is an attitude of love and respect rather than an automated compliance with authority. The vital question for parents is: What type of teaching and example can I give, what type of interaction can I promote, to facilitate this sort of reaction? How can I encourage this intelligent response in my children?

A system of discipline based on coercion and punishment is clearly not the answer. Obedience that does not involve reasoning and the participation of an autonomous will is not "honoring."

If we want to see in our children a response that springs from their own reasoning, their own intelligence and goodwill, then as early as possible, and as often as possible (in some cases, earlier and more often than we feel comfortable with), we must begin to appeal to those higher faculties, remembering that our goal is not to control but to encourage an attitude of honor.

Enlisting the will of our offspring does not involve an irresponsible surrender of parental authority. But it does mean that as soon as possible, we will let them choose in as many things as possible. We need to look for points in which they really can make a legitimate choice. Of course we would not ask a 2-year-old, "Would you rather have some orange juice or a glass of beer?" But if we look for such opportunities, and maybe even create them, there will be many points at which they can begin to exercise the power of choice. "Do you want your orange juice in the blue glass or in the one with flowers?" And before ever telling them no or "You have to do it my way," we will ask ourselves, "Does it really matter?" "What harm will it do?"

A few years ago popular psychology had a trend known as "transactional analysis." The letters "P-A-C," which stand for parent-adult-child, summed up a fundamental aspect of the theory. The idea was that every transaction, every exchange between two individuals, occurs on one of these three levels. A "parent" corrects, instructs, orders, and reprimands. "Pick up that shirt and put it in the closet." That, of course, is a "P" [for "parent"] intervention. The logical and appropriate response to these words will be a "C," or "child," reaction: "Aw, Mom, do I have to?" Or maybe even, "OK, Mom, I'll do it."

An "A" or "adult" intervention is one that considers the other person to be intelligent, willing to do the right thing, and capable of making a good decision. The natural response to an adult intervention is an adult reaction. The principle we are talking about here means that as early as possible and as often as possible, we should be engaging our children in adult-to-adult transactions.

When our son David was 8 years old, he had to catch the school bus every morning at 8:30. I found that waking him up on time was a monumental task that seemed to get worse as the days went by. Every morning I would go in and announce, "David, it's time to get up."

And his reply was something you would have to spell "Mmmmmm. Hmmmmmmmm."

A few minutes later: "David! I said it's time to get up. Didn't you hear me?"

"Mmmmmm. Hmmmmmmmm."

Still later, now thoroughly provoked, I would shout, "You get out of bed this very minute! If you don't get up right now, you're going to get it!"

At this point, with his eyes about 20 percent open, David would start to stir, while I tried to hurry him out of his pajamas and into his school clothes.

I had read about "P-A-C," but obviously it hadn't done me very much good at all.

Finally, one morning I went in and said, "Oh, David!"

"Yes?"

"What time are you going to get up?"

At this the blue eyes opened, and he looked at me seriously. "I don't know. What time is it?"

"It's quarter to seven."

"Oh, OK," he said, and immediately he sat up and started pulling off his pajamas.

I wish it were possible to claim that I never made the same mistake again, but the experience did serve to reinforce the principle: the very best plan for helping our children become responsible adults is to give them responsibility, to make them accountable for their own decisions as early as possible and as often as possible.

I had made it my job to get David to school on time, and by doing this I was taking the responsibility out of his hands. By putting it back where it belonged, I helped him prepare for life in the real world. And I aided him in keeping the fifth commandment, because honor is, above all else, an exercise of free will, a rational decision to have an attitude that will result in good and pleasant relationships with our parents first of all, and then with everyone else we deal with in life.

Does this mean that at times we will actually let them make wrong choices? In some cases there is no better way for them to learn than by having to reap the consequences of a wrong decision. And as the child's judgment and maturity grow, it will lead to a gradual increase in autonomy as well as in accountability.★

The Last Kiss

I don't remember the first time my mother kissed

me. It must have happened when I was a tiny baby, because she certainly kissed me many times while I was growing up. While I don't remember her first kiss, I do remember the last one.

The years go hurrying by, and every human relationship brings with it some stresses and strains. This is not horrible or disgraceful, but normal. But if we have in our hearts the overarching principle of honor, love will prevail. Then as the stresses threaten us, perhaps leading to pain and even bitterness, we should think about that last kiss, because it will surely come. What do you want to remember when you tell your parents goodbye for the last time?

A friend of mine told me that when his father grew old, the old man's mind was not always clear. Nevertheless, when the father's birthday came around, my friend decided to phone him. "Happy birthday, Dad," he said, "and God bless you."

That day the father's thoughts connected, because he instantly responded. "No, son. The blessing is for you. God bless you, because you have always honored me." Two months later my friend buried his father. What a comfort it was to him, then, to recall his father's words!

I have attended quite a few sad funerals, but never have I witnessed any more anguish and weeping than when regret made the sorrow of parting even more bitter.

So think about it while you still have the opportunity, while you can still do something or say something that will make a difference: Think about the last kiss, because it *will* come. Honor your father and your mother, and your days on earth will be not only longer but much more satisfying and filled with peace and joy and success.

_____

* "It is often personally inconvenient to allow children time

to debate alternatives, and it may be personally frustrating if their choice contradicts one's own preferences. If there is any selfish, sensitive 'pride' at stake, it is very hard for most adults to refrain from controlling children in an autocratic manner. Then, too, like any dictatorship, it looks 'more efficient,' to the dictator, at least. However, the effect on character is to arrest the development of rational judgment and to create such resentments as prevent the growth of genuinely altruistic impulses" (Robert Peck with Robert Havighurst et al., *The Psychology of Character Development* [New York: Wiley and Sons, 1960], p. 191).

GETTING CONTROL

The Sixth Commandment

You shall not murder.
        —*Exodus 20:13*

All of a sudden, *bang! bang! bang!* goes three or four guns. . . . The boys jumped for the river—both of them hurt—and as they swum down the current the men run along the bank shooting at them and singing out, 'Kill them, kill them!' It made me so sick. . . . I wished I hadn't ever come ashore that night to see such things."[1]

The passage has Huck Finn describing the savage murder of two teenage boys that resulted from an ongoing family feud. The story is fictional, but when Mark Twain wrote it in 1884, feuding was common in all the Southern states and especially in Appalachia, where rival clans fought each other with fierce intensity well into the twentieth century.[2]

Twain had one of his characters explain it in this way: "A man has a quarrel with another man, and kills him; then that other man's brother kills *him;* then the other brothers, on both sides, goes for one another; then the *cousins* chip in—and by and by everybody's killed off, and there ain't no more feud. But it's kind of slow, and takes a long time."[3]

The most famous of these bloody duels was the

long war between the Hatfields and the McCoys, who lived on opposite sides of the border between Kentucky and West Virginia. The origins of the feud are obscure, but according to some sources, the trouble began in 1878 with a dispute over the ownership of two razorback hogs. At its fiercest point, groups of 50 or more heavily armed men conducted raids across the state line. By the time the last killing took place in the mid-1890s, both families had been decimated.

Do you know why I like this illustration of breaking the sixth commandment? Because it's not related to anything I have ever done or even thought of doing. It doesn't make me feel at all guilty. In fact, I've lived my entire life up to now without even once crawling around the woods looking for someone to blow away.

Well . . . OK, maybe something like that *did* sort of cross my mind the other day when I was down at Wal-Mart. I'd never seen the parking lot so full. I drove up and down, back and forth, searching for a space. Finally one showed up clear down at the end of the row, so I headed for it. But . . . what do you think? . . . I was just about there, when along came this fellow and zoomed into it!

Hah! I tell you . . . for a few seconds I could just imagine myself leaping over there like Tarzan and grabbing him by the throat. But of course, I didn't actually do it. So that doesn't count, does it?

A Tiger Inside

We have a cat at home who is about as sweet and friendly as any that ever was. As soon as you sit down, she will come up and rub her whiskers on you a few times and then curl up with her little "motor" running. If you've ever had a friendly feline, you know how nice that is.

But let me ask you a question: What is the difference between a cat and a tiger? Do you know the real answer? It's their size.

Don't kid yourself. Your cat or mine—yes, that sweet little kitty—has the brain and all the instincts of a tiger, and is just as cold-blooded. If I were smaller and she were larger, she would be interested in me for the same reason she loves to watch the sparrows that land on our back porch.

When Jesus talked about the sixth commandment, He said: Your size doesn't count—if you have the mind and heart of a tiger, you're a tiger.

Here are His actual words:

"You have heard that the ancients were told, 'You shall not commit murder.' . . . But I say to you that everyone who is angry with his brother shall be guilty before the court; and whoever shall say to his brother, 'You good-for-nothing,' shall be guilty before the supreme court; and whoever says, 'You fool,' shall be guilty enough to go into the fiery hell" (Matthew 5:21, 22)

What does this mean? That when somebody provokes you, if you fail to take charge and control your feelings and actions, then the only difference between you and the Hatfields and the McCoys is your size. Because if you had lived where and when they did, you would have behaved exactly as they did.

The Perfect Solution

Most of us, of course, know the perfect solution to human relations problems: If people would just be nice to us, we would have no trouble at all being nice right back to them. But Jesus said: "Even the Gentiles do the same" (verse 47). The real question is: Can you be kind to someone who has hurt you? Can you really love someone who has wronged you?

It's not easy. In fact, some people think that Jesus' teaching on the sixth commandment is an extreme example, not intended to be actually obeyed, except maybe by a few saintly souls who live by themselves somewhere on a mountaintop. I heard a discussion of this once, and most of the people who spoke said that Jesus' teaching on the subject could not apply literally to people who live in the real world like the rest of us.

The Only Way

I strongly disagree. There are at least three important reasons Jesus' wisdom is a lot more than just a fluffy fantasy—that it's actually the only practical and sensible way to live.

1. *It's the only way to break the chain of violence.* Jesus' plan is best because the only alternative is the domino effect, an endless chain reaction of getting even. "An eye for an eye, a tooth for a tooth" is a recipe for disaster, because violence cannot be cured by more violence.[4] It took the Hatfields and the McCoys 20 years to figure that out. And it seems to be taking the Israelis and the Palestinians even longer.

We wonder why other people are so slow catching on, but this principle applies not only to family feuds and suicide bombers; it is also true when it comes to "mini-violence"—the verbal cutting and slashing that most of us engage in from time to time. Somebody has to make a conscious decision to break the vicious cycle, to swallow their pride and overlook the offense. And Jesus is telling His followers to be that somebody.[5]

A friend of mine who is a marriage counselor says that some of the most destructive fights start over trivial things:

"If you weren't so disorganized you could help

me find my keys."

"Don't tell me you've lost them *again!*"

And off they go! Neither one is willing to break the chain, so the situation quickly spirals out of control. The apostle James had precisely this in mind when he wrote: "See how great a forest is set aflame by such a small fire!" (James 3:5).

Passive-aggressive behavior, such as the silent treatment, turning our backs on someone, or pouting, is no less self-defeating than screaming. No matter what form it takes, unkind, mean-spirited behavior will only generate more of the same.

2. It's the only way to get control. In the second place, when we respond to ugliness with anger, hatred, and a desire for revenge, we are handing control over ourselves to someone else. We are letting them push our buttons and determine our feelings, attitudes, and reactions. Jesus wants to free us from this tyranny and give us back our autonomy along with our peace of mind.

Until we make the tough decision actually to do this, we are only reacting, not acting. Reactive (as opposed to active) behavior places us under the dominion of the cruel and thoughtless people who have been unkind to us. Jesus' method enables us to say to another individual: "You cannot force me to hate. I refuse to let you embitter my life. I am not willing to spend my days absorbed by anger."

In most cases reactive behavior is a weapon in a power struggle, usually wielded in a desire to control the other person. By being ugly to you, or by shunning you and withholding love, I am going to punish you for something I don't like, and force you to behave the way I want.

Active or assertive behavior and boundary setting

as practiced by a Christian have nothing to do with hatred and revenge, and much less with domination. They are an attempt not to control someone else, but to establish self-control. And they are a declaration not of independence, but of autonomy. Independence means withdrawal and turning our back on the other person, and may itself be a reactive behavior. Autonomy recognizes the value of interdependence. It does not reject a relationship in which we can help and willingly serve each other, but it demands respect for the God-given right to govern our own life.

To be truly assertive in Christian relations means more than to stop hating. It requires that we replace hatred with love. Jesus said:

> "Love your enemies,
> Do good to those who hate you,
> Bless those who curse you,
> Pray for those who mistreat you"
> (Luke 6:27, 28).[6]

When the apostle Paul takes up this theme, he puts it in practical terms:

> "If your enemy is hungry, feed him,
> and if he is thirsty, give him a drink;
> for in so doing you will heap burning
> coals on his head.
> Do not be overcome by evil,
> but overcome evil with good"
> (Romans 12:20, 21).

To actually love our enemies and do good to those unkind to us is the strongest and noblest expression of assertive behavior. And it places us in a position of strength, because it means we are refusing to play their game and descend to their level. Instead of being overcome, we are overcoming them.

3. *It's the only way to act responsibly*. By saying that we must not allow our enemies to determine our behavior and our attitudes, Jesus reminds us once again of our accountability. If we return anger for anger, ugliness for unkindness, it is our own decision to do this, because the power of choice is ours.

We like to justify reactive behavior by blaming someone else. It seems to make us feel better if we can spread the guilt around. "I'm acting this way because of the guy in the next cubicle." "I get upset easily because I'm like my grandmother (that's where I got this awful temper)." Or whatever.

A man I know became entangled in a family conflict that was ruining many lives. Having admired him as a Christian leader, I wondered how he could possibly stumble now. When I asked him, he said, "You have to realize what they did to us." Ever since Adam blamed Eve (Genesis 3:12) people have been giving this sort of answer.

We do not get to select our parents or how they raise us. And in most cases, neither can we choose our associates. The circumstances of life bring us together, and we are stuck with them. By making us accountable for how we react, Jesus wants us to accept responsibility and stop trying to justify our own bad behavior by pointing to someone else's.

The Word That Makes All the Difference

The golden rule has an often-overlooked word in it. It is "therefore," and it is the word that makes all the difference. Why? Because it connects us to the power line that lights up the golden rule and makes it actually work.

Of course, you remember the golden rule. It says: "All things whatsoever ye would that men should do to you, do ye even so to them" (Matthew 7:12, KJV).

The rule says what we should do, but the words that come just *before* the golden rule tell us why: "If you then, being evil, know how to give good gifts to your children, how much more will your Father who is in heaven give what is good to those who ask Him!" (verse 11). *"Therefore*, all things whatsoever ye would that men should do to you, do ye even so to them" (verse 12, KJV).

Why should we be good to other people? Because God is good to us. And why should the way others treat us not determine the way we treat them? Because God has poured out His love on us (Romans 5:5). "Just as the Lord forgave you," says the apostle, "so also should you" (Colossians 3:13). Can we really and genuinely forgive people who have hurt us, people who have deceived and betrayed us? Yes, because we have been forgiven so much. How could we possibly refuse to forgive someone else?[7]

Christians sometimes use the phrase "justification by faith." That is precisely what we are talking about here. The meaning of the complicated-sounding term is actually quite simple. It is that God, through Jesus Christ, has opened the doorway for our forgiveness, so that we can be forgiven without ever deserving it. Through this marvelous gift God pours out all of His other gifts on us as well. When we finally come to understand and accept this truth, overwhelming joy floods into the soul, and we have "the peace of God, which surpasses all comprehension" (Philippians 4:7).

Not just a good theory or a nice idea, what we have been examining is completely real, and it is what makes it possible for us, in turn, to offer heart-deep forgiveness to people who have hurt us, to be kind without having a selfish motive, and to love simply and sincerely without a hidden agenda.

One of the best-selling books of the twentieth century was Dale Carnegie's *How to Win Friends and Influence People*.[8] A human-relations manual based on principles of selfishness and manipulation, its message is: be nice to other people, compliment them, and make them feel good, because if you do, they will give you what you want and help you get ahead in life. The best we can hope for from such an approach is partially to hide or disguise our naturally selfish reactions, to paste over them a thin veneer of politeness. But just wait until someone really hurts us—then all such psychological strategies will blow up in our face, and we will turn back into tigers in a hurry.

True forgiveness is possible only when we are deeply aware of the depths of forgiveness we have received. When we see ourselves as forgiven sinners, our haughty arrogance against the people who have hurt us will melt away. Then we will begin to recognize these people who have hurt us as fellow travelers in life, individuals who, like ourselves, struggle against the power of an evil nature. Only then can compassion really begin to take the place of hatred, and true forgiveness begin to flow. There is no other way.

True Love Is a Gift From God

"Love is patient,
  love is kind
    and is not jealous;
  love does not brag
    and is not arrogant,
      does not act unbecomingly;
  it does not seek its own,

is not provoked,
    does not take into account a wrong suffered,
does not rejoice in unrighteousness,
    but rejoices with the truth;
bears all things,
    believes all things,
        hopes all things,
            endures all things"
                    (1 Corinthians 13:4-7).

True love is a divine gift. It comes only from God Himself.

---

[1] Samuel Clemens, *The Adventures of Huckleberry Finn* (New York: Harper & Row, 1884), p. 153.

[2] http://userwww.service.emory.edu/~dmcco01/McCoy/diversion.html.

[3] Clemens, p. 144.

[4] "An eye for an eye only ends up making the whole world blind" (Gandhi).

[5] "But I say to you, do not resist an evil person; but whoever slaps you on your right cheek, turn to him the other also" (Matthew 5:39). "A gentle answer turns away wrath, but a harsh word stirs up anger" (Proverbs 15:1).

[6] Similar to Matthew 5:38-44.

[7] Ephesians 4:32: "Be kind to one another, tender-hearted, forgiving each other, just as God in Christ also has forgiven you." Forgiveness means to stop hating, to let go of anger and a desire for revenge; it does not necessarily mean we must continue in a close relationship with the other person if this would place us in danger.

[8] Dale Carnegie, *How to Win Friends and Influence People* (New York: Simon and Schuster, 1936).

SOUL GLUE

The Seventh Commandment

You shall not commit adultery.
                    —Exodus 20:13

I have no idea what the experts would say is the most beautiful watch in the world, but my mind has no doubt at all. It would be the timepiece that always rode around in the lower left-hand pocket of my grandfather's vest. Made of pure gold, it was hinged on the back, and once in a while Grandfather would open the case and let me see the little escapement that was always ticking back and forth, back and forth, with each advance of the second hand. Other tiny wheels turned on their diamond bearings beside the mainspring that the old man wound every night just before going to bed. That watch was such an integral part of Grandfather that it seemed impossible to imagine him without it.

Once when I was 6 years old our family spent the weekend with Grandfather and Grandmother. Sunday morning I woke up early. Mom and Dad were still asleep, but I could hear a soft murmur of voices coming from the kitchen, so I went out and found my grandparents eating their oatmeal with warm applesauce and cream poured over it. After a good-morning hug, they put a bowl on the table for me, and I joined them. Grandfather's vest was unbuttoned, but the watch chain was visible, as usual, running from the loop where it was fastened and disappearing into the watch pocket.

With my elbows on the table and my chin on my hands, I looked at the old man's face and shared with him a wonderful thought that had just popped into my mind: "Grandfather," I said, "may I have your watch when you die?"

I don't remember if the blue eyes twinkled that time, as they often did. But his answer still echoes in my memory. "Yes," he said. "When I die, the watch will be yours."

A sense of awe filled me, and I was thrilled beyond words. I may not have even eaten breakfast before slipping away to whisper the wonderful news to Mother. To my amazement, she was horrified. "You didn't really ask him *that,* did you?"

Shrinking back, I nodded mutely. The joy of the moment instantly vanished. Mother's tone of voice made it clear I had done something really terrible.

"Can't you see that it sounds as if you were wishing he would die so you could have his watch?" she explained.

I was embarrassed and, of course, never mentioned the watch to Grandfather again. But he didn't forget. Two years later, just before he died, he said to Mother, "And remember, Zola, Loron is to have my watch."

After he was gone, Mother showed me the watch, then put it away for safekeeping in a little black box she kept high on the closet shelf. As the years went by, she would let me get it out once in a while to polish and wind it before putting it back. It was always a joy to see it and remember the love that it represented and the beautiful memories of Grandfather.

One day, when I was 14, instead of putting the

watch back, I put it in my pocket and said to Mother, "I'm old enough to take care of it now."

After quite a lengthy silence she replied, "I don't think it's a good idea, but you can decide."

The next morning Grandfather's watch went bouncing along toward school in the front pocket of my Levis. During the first part of the morning it was amazing how often I needed to check the time. Nothing like being the only kid in the room with a genuine gold pocket watch. I noticed the other students glancing my way from time to time, and I thought that maybe they would gather around at recess time to admire this wonderful timepiece. But, as usual, when the bell rang, the entire class made a headlong rush for the door, the boys grabbing their mitts as they ran.

I had forgotten that when we suspended the ball game on Friday, it was our team's turn at bat. It took about 35 seconds for everyone to get in place and yell, "OK, play ball!"

First, Bonell "Buzzy" Stevens struck out. Then Larry Fields got a hit that put him on second, and after that it was my turn. My reputation as strikeout king was seriously damaged when I hit the ball clear to the back field on the first pitch. By the time Glenn Hansen caught up with it and threw it to his brother Calvin, who was on first, I had barreled past there and was not far from second. I made a heroic dive and slid the rest of the way in, managing to touch the base about a tenth of a second before the ball thunked into Dal Cornforth's mitt.

Wow! Talk about pure adrenaline! Everyone was yelling at once. It was one of life's unforgettable moments, especially for a full-time Mr. Ziggy like me. I stood up, about an inch taller than before, and started to brush off the dust. Just then my hand came across something hard and flat and round in the right front pocket of my jeans. There it was, but for some reason it seemed strangely bent out of shape.

Oh, no . . . it couldn't be true! But it was. I still shudder to recall that terrible moment.

I knew, then, that I was the absolutely stupidest kid in the world. At 14 I didn't know much about the value of a gold pocket watch, but I knew how much I loved my grandfather, and he had entrusted it to me. And I had discovered that in a few seconds' time you can do something you will spend years—maybe the rest of your life—regretting.

That's what the seventh commandment is all about. It is about breaking something that is fragile and precious and very, very hard—sometimes impossible—to fix.

Some people would, of course, disagree. One of them was holding forth on a popular TV show not long ago. She began happily dropping names as she regaled her audience with details of her racy lifestyle. Before I could find the remote control she must have mentioned at least a half dozen famous people she claimed to have slept with.

For those who share this viewpoint, it's a brave new world, and its citizens say that a "revolution" and a great "liberation" have taken place, opening a doorway to boundless freedom and joy.

But they are wrong—and not because somebody invented a decree to spoil their fun. They are wrong because the seventh commandment expresses a fundamental law of life, a principle etched deeply in our hearts and minds. It is it based on the way we are wired, and we cannot break it without violating something deep inside.

One of the most famous passages in the Bible

helps us understand why this is so. I say "famous" because even people who have never opened the Bible
in their lives have heard of Genesis 2:22, 23.
Unfortunately, it sometimes gets used in the context
of a joke. But if we can leave that aside for a moment
and treat the passage with the respect it deserves, we
will discover that it has a deep meaning. It says:

*"The Lord God caused a deep sleep to fall upon the
man, and he slept; then He took one of his ribs and closed
up the flesh at that place. The Lord God fashioned into a
woman the rib which He had taken from the man, and
brought her to the man"* (Genesis 2:21, 22).

Adam's first words, the ones he spoke when he
saw this beautiful creature walking toward him, show
that he did get the point of what had happened. With
profound emotion Adam exclaimed, *"This is now bone
of my bones, and flesh of my flesh"* (verse 23).

It is clear that Adam's joy reflected the beginning
of their sexual relationship, because the record immediately adds:

"For this cause [that is, for this reason: because
woman was taken from man's body; because she is
bone of his bones and flesh of his flesh] *a man shall
leave his father and his mother, and shall cleave to his wife;
and they shall become one flesh"* (verse 24). Their once
again becoming one flesh is related to their having
originally been one flesh. It is God's design that
through the sexual relation flesh shall be joined to
flesh and spirit to spirit.

A well-known term in popular psychology describes the concept taught in Genesis 2:22-24: "identification." To "identify" with someone involves more
than to feel for them or to care about them. It means
that in some mysterious way we come to share their
identity—as if somehow we are them. Through identi-

fication we can see the world through their eyes, know their joy and their pain. This powerful force is at work when we cry at the end of a sad movie. Our tears flow because the actor has led us to identify with the character on the screen so that his or her loss becomes ours.

As Adam saw this beautiful creature now approaching, he had an overwhelming sense of identification in his heart. She was a part of him, for she had come from his own body. This is the reason for the incredible impact of the experience as he exclaimed, "This is now bone of my bones, and flesh of my flesh!" Then what could be more wonderful and natural for Adam than to hold her in his arms, feel her body pressing against his, and share with her the intense pleasure that God designed should accompany their glad rejoining?

God created and designed the sexual union to be a powerful instrument of identification and bonding. To say it another way: It is soul glue.

This is not merely a nice-sounding theory or a warm fuzzy idea. Science has discovered powerful chemicals that the body releases during sex. They intensify pair bonding. A hormone called oxytocin works directly on our brains to strengthen our relationship and identification, and its flow increases during intercourse. It means that God designed the physical aspect of the sex act to be part of the total intimacy of heart and mind that is marriage.

The apostle Paul also speaks of the bonding function of sex and says that it operates even when we may have no such intention. It means that, contrary to what some might wish to believe, it is not really possible to have sex and then walk away, believing that nothing has happened.

"Do you not know that the one who joins himself to a prostitute is one body with her?" Paul asked.

"For He says, 'The two will become one flesh'"
(1 Corinthians 6:16). You can climb out of bed, get
dressed, and leave, but something has happened. A
bonding has taken place, and you are taking something
with you. You are weaving an entangling web that, in
one way or another, will come back to haunt you.

Jesus also referred to the bonding function of
physical intimacy. "Have you not read that He who
created them from the beginning made them male and
female, and said, 'For this reason a man shall leave his
father and mother and shall be joined to his wife, and
the two shall become one flesh'? So they are no longer
two, but one flesh. What therefore God has joined
together, let no man separate" (Matthew 19:4-6).

Like Paul, Jesus is saying that the sexual relationship
is a divinely designed agency to make the joining of two
lives strong and permanent. It is heaven's way of ce-
menting together the two hearts, and they cannot afterward be torn apart without serious damage to both.

Safe Sex

One of the expressions used by those promoting
the sexual revolution is "safe sex." The phrase has led
millions of people to believe that there really is such a
thing as safety in a sleep-around lifestyle. It refers to
the idea that condoms can prevent disease. No doubt
they do help in this sense, but the protection they can
offer reduces but certainly does not eliminate the risk.
Furthermore, this myth rests on the idea that disease
is the only undesirable consequence of such behavior.
But the results of breaking the seventh commandment
are long-term and multifaceted.

Part of this same myth is the idea that "you have
to test-drive a car before you buy it." Sounds logical,
doesn't it? Living together, cohabitation, seems like a

risk-free way to check for compatibility. It should be an excellent method for achieving a perfect marriage.

The strange thing is that statistics show that it is the other way around: couples who begin their marriage in this way are almost twice as likely to divorce within 10 years compared to all first marriages.[1]

Furthermore, a recent study found that cohabiting couples reported rates of physical aggression in their relationships three times higher than those reported by married couples,[2] and the rate for severe violence was nearly five times as high as in married couples.[3] And the more sexually active they are before marriage, the more likely it is that one or both spouses will betray the other after the knot is tied.[4] It is hardly surprising that women involved in live-in relationships[5] report a very much higher rate of depression and a much lower rate of sexual satisfaction than do women in married relationships.[6]

The current explosion of STDs (sexually transmitted diseases) further challenges the concept of safe sex. A review of the scientific literature reveals that condoms fail to prevent the transmission of the HIV virus—which causes AIDS—between 15 percent and 31 percent of the time.[7] It should not surprise us, therefore, that while condom use has increased over the past 25 years, new cases and new kinds of STDs have grown even more rapidly.[8]

In the 1960s, before the beginning of the "sexual revolution," the main diseases transmitted by sexual contact were syphilis and gonorrhea, and they were believed to be disappearing because of the development of antibiotics. Today medical science has found more than 20 widespread types of STDs, with an average of more than 15 million new cases each year in the United States. Two thirds of all STDs occur in people 25 years of age or younger.[9] Each year 3 million teens contract an STD in the United States. Overall, at least one fourth of sexually active teens have become infected.[10]

The leading viral STD is the human papillomavirus (HPV), with 5.5 million new cases reported each year.[11] Another deadly scourge is *Chlamydia trachomatis,* which scars the fallopian tubes and is the fastest growing cause of infertility. Medical science still has no cure for viral diseases such as herpes and the human immunodeficiency virus (HIV), which causes AIDS. According to the U.S. Centers for Disease Control and Prevention, AIDS is a leading cause of death among 25- to 44-year-olds.

Merely reciting these numbers hardly gives a picture of what it means to have your life devastated by HPV or to watch a loved one die of AIDS. I can assure you it is a ghastly way to die.

What About the Children?

An even sadder result of the sexual revolution has been the fivefold increase in the number of children growing up in single-parent homes. According to the National Center for Health Statistics, out-of-wedlock births in the United States were 33 percent of all births in 2002, compared with 7 percent in 1960. This has happened in spite of the more than 1.3 million abortions performed annually in the U.S.

"There is not a single measure by which the children of this country are not doing worse" because of the change in sexual values, according to Patrick Fagan of the Heritage Foundation.[12] Children in single-parent homes are more likely to be abused by their parents; end up in jail; have to repeat a grade, drop out, or be expelled from school; use marijuana, cocaine, and tobacco; carry weapons; have serious emotional and behavioral problems; suffer from physical health problems; be sexually active; become unwed parents; or suffer depression or commit suicide.

All these are some of the more obvious results of the "freedom" and "liberation" that has taken place. It is certainly true that a radical change has occurred in the moral standards of some elements of society, but to describe it as a "liberation" or to promote it as an advance or improvement is like bragging about the freedom to smoke. And the annual number of people who are dying as a result of the sexual revolution far exceeds the annual number who die from smoking.

Getting Control

Jesus said that adultery begins where it ends: in the heart. "You have heard that it was said, 'You shall not commit adultery'; but I say to you that everyone who looks at a woman with lust for her has already committed adultery with her in his heart" (Matthew 5:27, 28).

He recognized that sexual arousal originates in the mind and that the mind is stimulated through the senses—by looking "at a woman with lust for her." Mental sex—unrestrained sexual fantasies—may seem like a pleasant and innocent pastime, but it is not. Looking at scenes that excite sexual desire and hearing or reading stories and descriptions of sex strongly stimulates such fantasies. So that's where the battle for self-control has to start.

It is common to talk about contamination of the environment by heavy industries. But another type of pollution is at least as widespread. That is the contamination of our environment by people who use sexually stimulating images on billboards, in print, on television, and in theaters everywhere.

A public debate rages today about sex education. One group says that we need to tell young people that the only safe sex is abstinence: "Just say no." Their opponents protest that this idea simply isn't working. That no matter how many times you tell them, they are going to do it anyway.

Both groups are right. Of course, young people are never going to be able to "just say no" if that's all we tell them. How could they, when bombarded day and night with highly stimulating images and sexual propaganda in the media? We need to explain to them—and let's drop the pretense: all of us need this, not just the teenagers—that sexual control starts where Jesus said it does: in our minds. If we allow ourselves to be taken to the edge time after time—if our plan of defense is to stop when we are the point of disaster—we are sure to fail.

Here is where the power of choice comes into play. Advertisers can publish stimulating pictures, but they cannot force us to keep looking at them or to buy their products. Songwriters can include vulgar lyrics in their music, but they cannot force us to listen or to focus our attention on their message. Nobody can oblige us, against our will, to continue watching an obscene video or TV program once we see where it is heading, or to keep on being friends with people who insist on pressuring us with their false values and tales about their affairs and conquests.

We were standing on the top of El Peñol, a gigantic sandstone monolith that rises abruptly hundreds of feet above the surrounding countryside in the country of Colombia. With some friends we had huffed and puffed our way up the 649 steps to the top.

To our great surprise, we saw no protective railing up there, no barriers or even any warning signs. The friendly guard told us that he had been on the job for more than 20 years.

"Has anyone ever gone over the edge?" I asked him.

"Yes," he said. "About 30."

Shocked, I asked, "Did all those people intend to jump, or was it an accident?"

"I don't know. We never could ask them." He seemed to be amused by this answer.

After chatting with the man for a while, we wandered around. The flat area on the top comprises about an acre. The curious thing is that there is no sudden precipice at the edge. At the sides it just starts to slope away gradually. In fact, it really doesn't seem all that dangerous.

While observing this, I got to thinking that it might be interesting to find out if a person could get close enough to the edge to be able to peek over. We could see for miles in all directions, but it would be a lot more exciting if we could look straight down, wouldn't it?

H'mm, OK, I think I'll just move a little closer to the edge. Hey, this is fun. But I still can't see very well. It's all right, Mom. Don't worry. I don't really plan to go all the way.

The top of El Peñol has no warning signs. But I'm glad that Jesus left us a clear warning in His teaching about the seventh commandment. Don't get even close to the edge, He said. Decide for yourself what your eyes will look at, what your mind will think about. Don't let the obscene advertisers and screenwriters determine the content of your thinking.

> "Whatever is true,
> whatever is honorable,
> whatever is right,
> whatever is pure,
> whatever is lovely,
> whatever is of good repute,

if there is any excellence and
if anything worthy of praise,
dwell on these things" (Philippians 4:8).

It is here that we must draw the line in the battle for purity. We can win the battle only by turning away from evil, by occupying the mind with positive and ennobling ideas, and by making God number one in our lives. "Thou wilt keep him in perfect peace, whose mind is stayed on thee: because he trusteth in thee" (Isaiah 26:3, KJV).

Whole Again

In a perfect society we could close this chapter right there, but we live in a broken and hurting world. Without doubt some of the people who read this are looking back on experiences they would rather forget.

One terrible day a group of men came to Jesus dragging a woman that they threw down at His feet like a dirty rag. "Teacher," they said, "this woman has been caught in adultery, in the very act" (John 8:4).

After Jesus had dealt with these hypocrites and they had left, He said to the woman, "Where are the people who were accusing you?"

Surprised, she opened her eyes and looked around. Then she replied, "There isn't anybody, Sir."

Jesus' question is for everyone who, like this woman, have found themselves overtaken by sin and filled with remorse and despair. He told her: "I don't condemn you either. Go, and sin no more."

"God did not send the Son into the world to judge the world, but that the world might be saved through Him" (John 3:17). "Therefore, there is now no condemnation for those who are in Christ Jesus" (John 8:1).

"I don't think it's a good idea," my mother commented when I wanted to take Grandfather's watch to school.

"Hey, I'm 14 now," I told her. "I know what I'm doing." And off I went.

When disaster struck, it seemed to me that I had broken something that was the most precious thing in the world, and that nothing could ever hurt so much. But I have since discovered that that wasn't true. There are things that are infinitely more precious than a gold watch, and breaking them hurts more than I could ever have imagined.

I have, since that day, known a lot more than 30 people who have gone over the edge with regard to the seventh commandment, and I have seen the hurt and far-reaching damage caused by what they did. But I have also witnessed healing and hope and restoration, and know that these are possible.

The damage I did that day to Grandfather's watch turned out to be reparable, and a few weeks later it was ticking away as faithfully as ever. In fact, I still have it today.

I praise God for the seventh commandment. It shows that He loves us and cares enough to warn us about the terrible danger. I am also thankful that that forgiveness and restoration are possible and freely available to all.

---

[1] Neil G. Bennett, Ann Klimas Blanc, and David E. Bloom, "Commitment and the Modern Union: Assessing the Link Between Premarital Cohabitation and Subsequent Marital Stability," *American Sociological Review* 53, no. 1 (February 1988): 127-138.

[2] Sonia Miner Salari and Bret M. Baldwin, "Verbal, Physical, and Injurious Aggression Among Intimate Couples Over Time," *Journal of Family Issues* 23, no. 4 (May 2002): 523-550.

[3] Kersti Yllo and Murray A. Straus, "Interpersonal Violence

Among Married and Cohabiting Couples," *Family Relations* 30:343.

[4] Andrew M. Greeley, *Faithful Attraction: Discovering Intimacy, Love and Fidelity in American Marriage* (New York: Tom Doherty Associates, 1991).

[5] Christina Hoff Sommers, *Who Stole Feminism? How Women Have Betrayed Women* (New York: Simon & Schuster, 1994), p. 251.

[6] These results were based on a survey of 1,100 people about their sexual satisfaction conducted by the Family Research Council and reported in William R. Mattox, Jr., "The Hottest Valentines: The Startling Secret of What Makes You a High-Voltage Lover," Washington *Post,* Feb. 13, 1994. Among the startling revelations of the survey was that "strictly monogamous women experience orgasm during sex more than twice as often as promiscuous women."

[7] Dr. Susan Weller, "A Meta-Analysis of Condom Effectiveness in Reducing Sexually Transmitted HIV," *Social Science and Medicine* 36, no. 12 (1993). See also National Institute of Allergy and Infectious Diseases, National Institutes of Health, Department of Health and Human Services, "Summary of Scientific Evidence on Condom Effectiveness for Sexually Transmitted Disease (STD) Prevention," July 20, 2001.

[8] Centers for Disease Control and Prevention, "Tracking the Hidden Epidemics 2000: Trends in STDs in the United States," at http://www.cdc.gov/nchstp/od/news/RevBrochure1pdftoc.htm.

[9] Shepherd Smith and Joe S. McIlhaney, M.D., "Statement of Dissent on the Surgeon General's Call to Action to Promote Sexual Health and Responsible Sexual Behavior," issued by the Medical Institute of Sexual Health (Austin, Texas), June 28, 2001; American Social Health Association (Triangle Park, N.C.), "STD Statistics," at http://www.ashastd.org/stdfaqs/statistics.html.

[10] Alan Guttmacher Institute, *Sex and America's Teenagers* (New York: Alan Guttmacher Institute, 1994), pp. 19, 20.

[11] American Social Health Association, "STD Statistics."

[12] See Patrick F. Fagan et al., *The Positive Effects of Marriage* (Heritage Foundation, 2002).

SOMETHING FOR NOTHING

The Eighth Commandment

You shall not steal.
—*Exodus 20:15*

There's a man in the window!"

I don't ever recall being jerked from sleep so abruptly as when I heard my wife say those words. We were in Mexico City for a brief vacation with our son David. On that mild summer evening we had drifted off to sleep with the window of our guest room open to catch the breezes. It was a third-story window that opened onto an inner courtyard, so it had seemed safe enough.

For a few long seconds I stared at the vague shadow in the window. It can be difficult to know what you are seeing at night. So what was it, really? A slight resemblance, maybe, but I could think of no logical way that it could actually be a man.

Then, just as I was about speak a few words of re-assurance to Ruth Ann, the shadow began to move. It was indeed a man, and he was definitely coming right on in.

Now, before going any further, I would like to stop and ask a question: What do you think that person wanted?

Does it seem like an absurd question to you? It's not hard to guess he was planning to relieve us of some of our possessions. But by asking I want to open the issue a bit more, and maybe to explore the meaning of thievery itself.

Here is a list of some of the most common kinds of stealing. You will notice that our man in the window has lots of company, people who share his intentions and mentality, most of whom are not nearly as much despised as he is by polite society.

1. *Theft*. This is the first kind that comes to mind when we talk about stealing. Our visitor would fit into this category. The traditional kind of robbery, it means to take something without the owner's consent, to borrow something and not return it, to owe something and not pay. That's theft, plain and simple.

2. *Illegal copying*. Making a copy that deprives the author, artist, and publisher of their right to compensation, whether it involves printed matter or material in digital or any other format.

3. *Plagiarism*. Presenting another person's work or answers as your own in order to get a grade or other benefit for yourself.[1]

4. *Information manipulation*. Achieving personal gain or advantage through lying, exaggerating, or telling less than the whole truth. It includes fraud, swindle, scam, or any sort of deception that results in injury or loss to another person, and also the use of insider information to take advantage of someone.

5. *Slander, defamation*. Depriving others of their reputation and good name, and the esteem, love, and respect they have a right to enjoy. It may also rob them of employment and other things by false accusations and misinterpretation of their motives and conduct.

6. *Slacking off on the job*. "Goofing off," being unjustifiably idle on company time, doing less than your best at work, arriving late and leaving early.

7. *Waste.* Squandering or misusing material or time that belongs to another person.

8. *Carelessness.* This includes neglect and other forms of irresponsible behavior that result in loss to another person.

9. *Overcharging.* Profiteering, price gouging, charging an excessive amount for something when the buyer has no other choice but to accept it.

10. *Underpayment.* Paying less than the fair value for something when the seller is at a disadvantage. Or it may involve less than fair wages when the employee is desperate for work.[2]

11. *Abuse or neglect of children.* Parents who do not properly care for their children are stealing from them something that is theirs by right. This may be done by workaholic or absentee parents as well as by parents who commit mental, physical, or sexual abuse.

12. *Marital unfaithfulness.* A spouse who is abusive or unfaithful or who walks away from the marriage deprives the faithful mate of rights granted by marriage vows, including sexual satisfaction, economic support, cooperation in raising and educating the children, etc. Adultery is one of the worst kinds of stealing—it is taking something to which we have no right and that belongs exclusively to someone else.[3]

13. *Kidnapping, slavery, wrongful imprisonment* (Deuteronomy 24:7). Contrary to what you may believe, this is not uncommon today. According to United Nations statistics, at least 600,000-800,000 people, mostly women and children, are annually trafficked across borders worldwide, including 14,500-17,500 persons into the United States.[4] It can involve false imprisonment. Even if only 1 percent of prisoners in the United States are not guilty, that is still more than 10,000 innocent people behind bars. Most experts believe that the actual per-

centage is higher, and in some countries it may be considerably greater.

14. *Withholding tithe.* This deprives someone of an opportunity to hear the gospel, to find peace and hope and a better life. Faithful returning of tithe might make it possible to reach others with the news of God's love (Malachi 3:8).

You may think of other types of stealing.

Now, let's ask again: What do you think the man who crept into our window that night in Mexico City wanted?

He had in mind exactly the same thing that all other people on this list want: something they have not earned, something that was not theirs and to which they had no right. The robber in our window sought to get *something for nothing*.

The Sweat Component

The first biblical rule against stealing appears in Genesis 3:19. It declares: "By the sweat of your face you shall eat bread."

Here is how the apostle Paul puts it: "He who steals must steal no longer; but rather he must labor, performing with his own hands what is good, so that he will have something to share with one who has need" (Ephesians 4:28).

Did you notice that this Bible prescription for stealing has two parts? The first is self-support: "He who steals . . . must labor, performing with his own hands what is good." We are to earn what we get, to acquire it by exchanging value for value.

The Reformation of the sixteenth century was a powerful religious and theological movement, but it was also a social upheaval that shook European society to its foundations. The changes it brought about touched every aspect of human life, and benefited even the people who opposed the religious ideas that it supported.

The showcase for the Reformed thinking, the place where it was most closely applied to daily life, was the city of Geneva under the administration of John Calvin.

Poor people lived in Geneva. As the Reformation went forward and the fires of the Inquisition blazed, Geneva came to be flooded with refugees, and most of them arrived with nothing. But the city took care of them. Other individuals were elderly, infirm, or alone, and Geneva also made provision for them. Civic leaders divided the city into wards, and deacons were responsible for knowing and caring for the needs of the poor. In addition to direct assistance, people could receive interest-free loans and free elementary education for their children.

But while poverty was not condemned, idleness was. Calvin emphasized the dignity of labor. Considering hard work a virtue and laziness a public offense, he did not believe that people who are unwilling to work had a right to profit from the efforts of those who do.[5] Calvin liked to quote Psalm 128:2: "When you shall eat the fruit of your hands, you will be happy and it will be well with you." And Proverbs 10:4: "The hand of the diligent maketh rich" (KJV).[6]

As the government under Calvin's rule applied such biblical principles, the results soon proved their value. Within a few years Geneva was the most prosperous city in Europe. It was by far the cleanest and probably the healthiest, too, because community regulations required home and business owners to keep their premises clean and to sweep and scrub the street in front of their property. It is hardly surprising that in this environment theft and violent crime were practically unheard-of.

God designed the sweat component of life to be a blessing—to bring relief from stress, to add years and good health to the body, and peace and order to the mind.

"Excuse Me, Please"

We never did know the philosophy of the man who came in through our window that night in Mexico City. After I spoke to him in a decidedly unwelcoming tone of voice and David made a sound that was a cross between a banshee and the Lion King, he paused and said very politely in English, "Excuse me, pleese." Then carefully and deliberately he backed out and retreated, climbing up a drainpipe to reach the roof and descend the other side.

Wherever I have told this story, people have reacted in amazement: "What! A Mexican thief in Mexico City who could speak English?"

But maybe it shouldn't be so surprising. The individuals who engage in this profession are generally not stupid. In fact, a lot of them consider themselves smarter than the rest of us. Why work for minimum wages at McDonald's when you can get more money for less effort?

That's a good question. In fact, let's broaden it a bit more. Why should I slave away for hours on a term paper when it takes about five minutes to get one from the Internet? What sense does it make to pay $75 for software when my buddy is offering me a copy for free? And why not spend my time chatting by the water cooler or on the Internet at work? They aren't paying me what I deserve anyway. And the government? . . . Hey! they rake in billions every day, so why shouldn't I cheat a little bit on my tax report? Yes, why not? That's what smart people do, isn't it? The man who told me he was on the welfare list in two states felt he was a lot brighter than people who have to get up every morning and be at work by 9:00.

The Worst Day of a Man's Life

Thomas Jefferson had a different idea. He said: "The worst day of a man's life is the day he sits down and plans how he can get something for nothing." Jefferson was thinking not of the damage that burglars can do when they crawl in through our windows at night, but of the devastating effect this mind-set has on those who indulge in it. This is the essential reason for the warning given in the eighth commandment.

The "smart" people who take this path to easy street are making a terrible trade-off. They are bartering away their personal integrity, their values and self-esteem, and what are they getting in exchange?

1. Dishonesty is destructive to our sense of personal satisfaction and self-respect. It may be possible to conceal a dishonest act from other people, but we can never hide it from ourselves. We may have gotten the grade or something else we wanted, but in the process we have given away the wholesome joy that comes from a sense of accomplishment, the satisfaction of personal achievement and a job well done.

2. The something-for-nothing syndrome has a depraving, degrading effect on the character. It is an addictive behavior that can degenerate into serious mental health problems. Gambling and shoplifting addictions affect millions of people, destroying lives and marriages and costing society billions of dollars. Sexual addictions and workaholism are closely related and can be equally destructive and difficult to over-

come. Even the people who practice their dishonesty in ways that society approves or overlooks may be causing serious damage to themselves and others.

3. Something for nothing degrades our relationships with other people. Dishonesty pits one person against another, because there really is "no such thing as a free lunch."[7] Somebody had to pay for it. If I am getting it at their expense, this pits me against them. Furthermore, after any dishonest act, it is natural to dehumanize and degrade the victims in an attempt to convince ourselves in our own minds that they deserved what we did to them.

The something-for-nothing syndrome turns other people into objects to manipulate for our gain. We may hide this truth under one or more layers of politeness, but in the final analysis our motto is: Me first. And the question of the day becomes: What's in it for me? How can this person serve my interests? I will be nice to you, compliment and praise you for what I hope to get out of you, but only to the degree that you can supply my wants and advance my interests.

Altogether too many people enter marriage and decide to divorce on precisely these terms.

The Love Component

As we have seen, the first element in the biblical prescription for dishonesty is self-support. The second is generosity. The text says: "He must labor, performing with his own hands what is good, *so that he will have something to share with him who has need*" (Ephesians 4:28).

The opposite of stealing is giving. It is impartially reaching out to others, serving them with love, expecting nothing in return.

Jesus' parable of the good Samaritan is a perfect illustration of this principle. Robbers attacked a traveler and seized everything he had. They thought they had taken his life, as well, when they discarded him at the side of the road (Luke 10:30-36).

What the good Samaritan did was just the opposite. Whereas the thieves had taken away, the Samaritan gave. Never mind that he exposed himself to danger or that if circumstances had been reversed, the traveler might not have given him a second glance. And much less was he hoping that the wounded man would in some way reciprocate and repay him for his efforts. One thing alone moved this man: compassion—which is another way of saying: love. Because he loved, he gave.

Stealing is not the only expression of selfishness, but it is one of the crudest and most direct. But while stealing takes away, love gives. Love is the antonym of selfishness, and its remedy. Although love does not necessarily cure selfishness in the one who is loved, it certainly does in the one who loves.

Without the love component, the sweat component (that is, earning your own way and paying for what you get) is not really a complete cure for the something-for-nothing syndrome. In fact, it can lead us to compare ourselves with others and to harbor pride and greed. To personal effort and integrity we must add compassion, impartial love that gives of itself in service to others. As Paul says, we are to "labor, performing with [our] own hands what is good, *so that [we] will have something to share with [those who have] need.*"

Trying to Get Something for Nothing From God

The most dangerous kind of something for nothing is the kind we try to bring into our relationship with

God. I have to admit that here we venture into a treacherous area in which it is easy to get confused, because the Bible says that salvation is a "free gift."[8] In fact, this is the essential message of the gospel. Good works never earned salvation for anyone, and never will.

The trouble comes when some people take this to mean that good works don't matter. Or that we can have a cafeteria-style religion, observing those commandments we like and considering others abolished by grace. Can we tell people we are saved while continuing to overlook what God has told us in the Ten Commandments or in any other part of the Bible?

John MacArthur answers this question eloquently: "The gospel in vogue today holds forth a false hope to sinners. It promises them they can have eternal life yet continue to live in rebellion against God. Indeed it encourages people to claim Jesus as Savior yet defer until later the commitment to obey Him as Lord. It promises salvation from hell but not necessarily freedom from iniquity. It offers false security to people who revel in the sins of the flesh and spurn the way of holiness. By separating faith from faithfulness, it teaches that intellectual assent is as valid as wholehearted obedience to the truth."[9]

Dietrich Bonhoefffer called it "cheap grace." Not long before his death at the hands of the gestapo, he wrote:

"Cheap grace is the preaching of forgiveness without requiring repentance, baptism without church discipline, Communion without confession. . . . Cheap grace is grace without discipleship, grace without the cross, grace without Jesus Christ, living and incarnate."[10]

Grace is the heart of the gospel. It means that we can come to Jesus just as we are, without waiting to be good enough. We don't have to creep in through the back door, even when our report card is marked all over with the record of our failures and mistakes. Incredible as it may seem, the gospel tells us that we can approach God "boldly" (Hebrews 4:16, KJV).

But does this amazing grace mean that we can just as boldly go on sinning? The apostle Paul knew that it was what some people were thinking, so he asked them: "What shall we say then? Are we to continue in sin that grace may increase?" (Romans 6:1).

The most eloquent answer I have heard to this question comes from a thoroughly uneloquent man. Berkley Jones was an embittered and dangerous criminal, considered incorrigible by the Oregon state penal authorities. But one glorious day Jesus found a place in his heart, and when that happened, everything changed.[11] Not long afterward, Berkley wrote that recently someone had asked if he had ever felt a desire to go back to the life he had before he had met Jesus. This seemed to him to be the most absurd question in the world. He compared it to a man drowning in a cesspool being pulled out, then wanting to turn around and jump right back in, knowing perfectly well that there was nothing in there but rottenness and death.

Why would anyone prefer the cesspool when Jesus offers health and healing for our souls? The answer to "cheap grace," Bonhoeffer declared, is "Jesus Christ, living and incarnate."

This is a good place to recall again a promise I made in the opening chapter. That was never to ask you to accept blindly anything I have to say about this extremely important subject, but, on the contrary, to give you ample opportunity to verify and prove for yourself the validity of the principles set forth. And that verification is in the application. I do hope you have already begun to test these principles in your life, to make them a part of your universe. If you have, you already know what I am talking about, because the results are immediate and deeply satisfying.

---

[1] Research by the Center for Academic Integrity confirms that cheating is a widespread and growing problem on many campuses: http://www.academicintegrity.org.

[2] James 5:4: "Behold, the pay of the laborers who mowed your fields, and which has been withheld by you, cries out against you; and the outcry of those who did the harvesting has reached the ears of the Lord of Sabaoth."

[3] Joseph stated this principle in his reply to Potiphar's wife (Genesis 39:7-9).

[4] http://www.state.gov/g/tip.

[5] "For even when we were with you, we used to give you this order: if anyone is not willing to work, then he is not to eat, either" (2 Thessalonians 3:10).

[6] See William McCornish, "Calvin and the Poor," at http://www.warc.ch/24gc/cts/cts11.pdf.

[7] A saying popularized by science fiction writer Robert A. Heinlein.

[8] Romans 6:23: "For the wages of sin is death, but the free gift of God is eternal life in Christ Jesus our Lord."

[9] *The Gospel According to Jesus* (Grand Rapids. Zondervan, 1994), pp. 201, 202.

[10] *The Cost of Discipleship* (New York: Macmillan Publishing Co., 1963), pp. 42-44.

[11] Story told by Rose Slaybaugh in *Escape From Death* (Nashville: Southern Publishing Assn., 1953), pp. 113-143.

MORE THAN LIFE ITSELF

The Ninth Commandment

You shall not bear false witness against your neighbor.
—Exodus 20:16

One day around 1870 the manager of a large railroad in the eastern United States was surprised to receive a visit from one of his competitors.

Without wasting time on formalities, the man described a scheme by which the two companies could deceive a mutual competitor and put him out of business. The result would be worth millions of dollars in revenues for both companies.

The manager immediately pulled back from his desk and said, "Sir, that is not how we do business here. Furthermore, I am sure Mr. Vanderbilt [the owner] would not approve."

"I can't see why we should need to trouble the old gentleman about this," the man continued. "And—did I mention?—we have a draft for $10,000 in your name, if you see fit to use it."

"Sorry," the manager replied firmly. "It's out of the question."

"H'mmm, did I say $10,000? I must have misspoken. Actually, the draft is for twice that amount."

At this the executive edged still farther away from his desk and glared at his visitor, who, mistaking the reason for his reaction, added hastily: "However, it's just possible we could find a way to make it $30,000."

Springing to his feet, the manager roared, "Get out of my office! Get out this instant, you scoundrel, before I have you thrown out!"

After the visitor had retreated, the secretary, who had overheard the entire conversation, came in. He found his boss sitting at his desk, wiping his brow.

"Sir," he said, "I can't begin to tell you how much I admire you for . . ."

"Don't say it," his boss replied, holding up his hand. "The truth is, I had to get him out of here in a hurry. He was getting close to my price."

What do you think? Is it true, as this story seems to imply, that everybody has a price? Perhaps I should approach it another way: How much is *your* honesty worth? Would *you* sell out for $30,000?

Now, let's be honest (that's what we're talking about, isn't it?): under the right circumstances a lot of people would sell out for less.

We All Do It, Don't We?

What about telling a lie . . .

. . . to avoid embarrassment? "I'm really sorry, Mrs. Hendley. We couldn't finish your job last night because our whiz machine was broken." (Actually, we forgot all about it.)

. . . to keep from hurting someone's feelings? "Thank you for sending those muffins. They were delicious." (We took one bite and threw the rest away.)

. . . to save money? "Oh no, Mr. Customs Inspector, we didn't buy anything on our trip abroad." (Just some silver plates. They're right there under the towels.)

. . . to get a better grade? "I did finished the term paper, Dr. Shivers, but the electricity went out just before I could save it to the hard drive." (Modern version of "My dog ate it.")

Hey, but wait! We were talking about lies that would ruin a railroad. That's not the same as common, garden-variety untruths. These are innocent little everyday prevarications. Not a big deal, right?

In fact, Anglican priest Joseph Fletcher wanted to take it even further. He formulated an ethical system that would legitimize most "conventional" lies. In his famous *Situation Ethics*,[1] Fletcher taught that the "right" action in any given case depends on the situation. Even a whopper may be justified, he claimed, if the motive is right.

It is easy to understand why this way of thinking has influenced millions of people. Popular spinoffs from Fletcher's ideas have made lying more than just socially acceptable—a lot of people even consider it essential.[2]

The Problem With Lying

It is not hard to discover that the Bible disagrees sharply with this slippery ethic. King Solomon says that "lying lips are an abomination to the Lord" (Proverbs 12:22). An "abomination" is something hateful and disgusting.

The apostle Paul is no less emphatic. He puts liars on the same list with people "who kill their fathers and mothers," "murderers," "immoral men," and "kidnappers" (1 Timothy 1:9, 10). He considers them "lawless and rebellious" (verse 9). The book of Revelation joins in the chorus, warning us solemnly that "no one who practices abomination and lying" will have a part in God's eternity (Revelation 21:27). We could add dozens of other passages throughout the Bible that echo the same radical point of view.

What's All the Fuss About?

What's so bad about a little lie now and then? Why does the Bible insist so much on telling the truth?

Consider the following:

1. *Lying destroys the freedom and dignity of our victims* because it is always manipulative. By lying to someone, we take away their ability to choose rationally, to make a decision and form an opinion based on accurate information. It means that we are treating people with contempt, as objects to fool and deceive for our own selfish ends.

2. *Lying damages the personal freedom of the people who engage in it,* because they quickly become entangled in the sticky web of their own deception and manipulation. Abraham Lincoln said: "No man has a good enough memory to make a successful liar." Truth tellers do not have to strain to avoid the pitfalls they have set for themselves, but liars keep digging in deeper as they lie more and more, attempting to cover their previous falsehoods.

3. *Lying destroys trust.* It is sometimes possible to deceive other people, but usually not for long. Distrust and suspicion increase exponentially when a lie is discovered. Nobody trusts a liar. And it is also true that no one is more suspicious than a liar. People who lie naturally don't trust other people. They assume that they are just like them.

4. *Lying damages the liar's sense of self-worth.* Even if it is possible to deceive other people for a while, it is very much harder to fool ourselves. I may be able to pull the wool over your eyes, but I have done serious damage to myself, because I know that I am a fake and a hypocrite.

5. *Lying destroys our relationship with God.* This may be the least concern of someone squirming in an effort to get out of trouble. But in the end it is the most devastating effect of all. Let us look at this further.

The God Who Is

The people "may say to me 'What is His name?'" Moses inquired. "What shall I say to them?" (Exodus 3:13).

"Ehyeh asher Ehyeh," said the voice from the burning bush. "I AM WHO I AM." "Thus you shall say to the sons of Israel, 'I AM has sent me to you'" (verse 14). With this, God was identifying Himself by His most fundamental characteristic: He is the one who is.

The apostle John tells us that "in the beginning, the Word," who was God, was already present (John 1:1). The text does not say in the beginning of what, because it doesn't matter. Nor does it explain when that beginning occurred—that doesn't matter either. Whatever it was, it had a beginning, but God did not. Whenever it was, He was already there. He is the self-sufficient, unchanging, ever-present one.

For many centuries the Rock of Gibraltar (1,398 feet high) has been a symbol of all that is solid and reliable. I grew up in the shadow of Pikes Peak, a mountain that is solid granite, reaching 14,110 feet into the sky. But even these mighty metaphors fade into insignificance when we compare them to the character of God.

The Hebrew word most often translated as "truth" is *emeth.* In everyday speech "truth" refers to the facts. "I am telling you the truth" means "I am telling you the facts as I know them." But the biblical idea of *emeth* is not merely one's perception of things—it is the intrinsic nature of things as they are. It is not just something we tell, but rather what is.

Psalm 31:5 refers to the God of *emeth,* the God of truth (see also Jeremiah 10:10). This does not mean simply that He is a truth-telling God. He is truth, reality itself. All other reality derives from Him and is borrowed from Him.

The devil, said Jesus, "does not stand in the truth because there is no truth in him. Whenever he speaks a lie, he speaks from his own nature, for he is a liar and the father of lies" (John 8:44). Lying and falsehood are the antitheses of God. They are anti-God, and when we indulge in them, we are blotting Him out of our sky. And if we persist in this habit, we are ripping His image out of our souls.

The Time of the Big Lie

Jesus warned that the time is coming when millions of people will be overwhelmed by the most powerful and sophisticated deception ever known. Highly convincing religious leaders will "show great signs and wonders, so as to mislead, if possible, even the elect" (Matthew 24:24; see also 2 John 7). We call this movement "anti-Christ," because Jesus' mission from the beginning was to tell the truth about God (John 18:37).

The apostle Paul also speaks about this powerful end-time deception. Notice especially the verses in which he tells us the reason it will sweep so many people away. Antichrist, "the man of sin" (2 Thessalonians 2:3, KJV), will come with "all power and signs and false wonders . . . for those who perish, because they did not receive the love of the truth so as to be saved" (verses 9, 10).

So why are millions of people going to be over whelmed by the last great deception? Because they do not *love* the truth.

When we studied the sixth commandment, we learned that "Do not murder" requires that we must actively love our enemies. Now here, in the ninth commandment, we discover that "Do not lie" demands that we must love the truth.

Can you think what this means? What do people who *love* the truth do?

If we love the truth, we will search for it. It will seem important to us to discover it. We will take the time and make the effort necessary (John 5:39). Daily Bible study and prayer for understanding will be a normal part of our lives (Acts 17:11). Like the psalmist, we will pray, "Lead me in thy truth and teach me" (Psalm 25:5, KJV).

Jesus is truth (John 14:6). His whole life was a revelation of the truth about God (John 18:36, 37). So if we love truth we will study the meaning of His words and deeds.

If we love the truth, we will value it. Jesus told a story about a man plowing who found his plowshare suddenly striking something hard. It was an ancient box filled with treasure. The man immediately sold all that he had and bought the field. Jesus said that the man did so with "joy" (Matthew 13:44). Why the joy? The answer is obvious, isn't it? He was happy because he had recognized the value of what he had found. The man knew that the treasure was worth far more than anything he already owned.

The "field" in Jesus' story represents the Bible, the Word of God. The treasure is the truth it that contains. If we really love truth, we will experience this same joy as we study Scripture and discover the beauty of its teachings (1 Corinthians 13:6). It will be more precious to us than silver or gold (Job 28:15; Proverbs 16:16), even more than life itself. In the words of the great Reformation hymn:

> "Let goods and kindred go,
>   this mortal life also;
> The body they may kill;
>   God's truth abideth still." [3]

Thousands of people in those days proved the sincerity of these words as the fires of religious persecution blazed.

If we love the truth, it will transform our lives. The Bible makes it plain that something is not really truth to us unless it makes a difference in how we live and how we behave (Galatians 5:7; Romans 2:8).

And finally, *if we love the truth, we will be eager to share it.* Once we have seen the beauty of truth and experienced its power (1 Peter 1:22), we will be excited about it, and it will seem natural for us to share it.

Jesus said that this was His mission in life—He came as a witness to truth (John 18:37). When He left, He commissioned all His followers to be witnesses in His stead, to carry on the same task (Acts 1:8).

The No-Lie People

The prophecy about the end-time has a note of immense encouragement for all of us. It says that not everyone will be overwhelmed by the big lie. John the revelator saw in vision a group of individuals living in the last days who "follow the Lamb wherever He goes" (Revelation 14:4). They follow Jesus, who is the truth, and that following means unreserved obedience.

The prophecy then adds that "no lie was found in their mouth" (verse 5). If no lie was found in their mouth, it means that the truth was there instead. They are people who value the truth enough to look for it, and they have discovered it. Having found it, they want to share it, because the prophecy says it is "in their mouths"—they want to talk about it. What they had encountered changed their lives, and now they are not willing to keep it selfishly to themselves. As a result they become fearless witnesses for God and for truth in the midst of overwhelming deception.

At this point history will have come full circle. These followers of the Lamb will be worthy successors of the first Christians who had to stand against the powerful pressures of the political correctness and groupthink of their day. When the religious leaders brought in the apostles and had them flogged, the record says: "They went on their way . . . rejoicing that they had been considered worthy to suffer shame for His name. And every day, in the temple and from house to house, they kept right on teaching and preaching Jesus as the Christ" (Acts 5:41, 42).

The early Christians, like the people who will walk with the Lamb in the last days, understood the meaning of the ninth commandment. For them, not bearing false witness meant bearing a fearless witness to the truth. And in this way they were worthy followers of Jesus, who said, "I am the way, and the truth, and the life" (John 14:6).

---

[1] Joseph Fletcher, *Situation Ethics* (London: SMC Press, 1966).

[2] This is not intended as a comprehensive statement on Fletcher's ideas. It is fairly common in ethical studies to present examples of situations in which a lie might be justified: to save someone from the Nazi gas chambers, for example. The problem is that too many people might extrapolate from these extreme situations to make lying acceptable anytime we find ourselves in an uncomfortable or embarrassing predicament.

[3] From Martin Luther, "A Mighty Fortress."

OUT-OF-ORDER ATTACHMENT

The Tenth Commandment

You shall not covet your neighbor's house;
you shall not covet your neighbor's wife or his
male servant or his female servant or his ox or
his donkey or anything that belongs to your neighbor.
                                    —*Exodus 20:17*

I must have been about 14 when it happened. I was going about business as usual one day when a beautiful young girl went strolling by. What impressed me most about the incident was not her charming smile or lilting walk, but the fact that she carried in her hand a portable radio from which poured the swirling melody of a Strauss waltz.

Talk about love at first sight! From that moment on, I was definitely convinced that happiness and fulfillment in life consisted in my becoming the owner of a portable radio.

Now, in those ancient times such items were not imported from China and sold for a dollar and a half at the local discount store. Furthermore, the fragile state of my economy made it clear that acquiring one would not occur overnight; but, most definitely, it would happen. From that moment on, all my odd jobs and Christmas or birthday gifts were dedicated to the radio fund. Finally, one supremely happy day I counted out $43 and went downtown to buy *the* radio.

No one was in the house when I got back, so I went to my room to do my homework. Not *just* to do homework, of course. While I worked on algebra, "Don't Let the Stars Get in Your Eyes" created a dreamy ambience in the background. Ah, bliss! What could be nicer than that?

Before long I needed a glass of water, so I headed for the kitchen. And the radio? Hey! It was a portable. You didn't think it was going to stay behind in my room, did you?

"Glow, little glow-worm, fly of fire!" sang the radio, pressed tightly against my ear. My eyes were half closed and my feet moved along in time to the rhythm—that is, they were moving until the instant my left foot hooked against the table leg. One second I was skipping and hopping, and the next I was taking a nosedive toward the floor. My hands flew out reflexively. They succeeded in saving my face from crashing into the countertop, but the radio . . . Alas! the radio! It described a neat parabolic arc as it flew through the air and disintegrated on the linoleum. End of song.

My father was gentle when he came home a few hours later and found out what had happened, but even so, he couldn't resist saying, "Turned out to be a pretty expensive radio, didn't it, son?" Indeed, it had.

I wish I could tell you I learned a profound lesson then and there, and never forgot it. Unfortunately, that was not the case. But the message was plain enough, and it would have been the same even if the radio hadn't shattered that day: *Happiness that comes from things tends to be short-lived.*

Jesus said it a lot better: "Take heed and beware of covetousness, for one's life does not consist in the abundance of the things he possesses" (Luke 12:15, NKJV).

When the "New" Wears Off

Mother used to say, "Wait till the 'new' wears off." If my radio hadn't broken that day, the "new"—the novelty and excitement of ownership—would have faded anyway. Maybe not the first day, or the second, but it would have still happened. That is a law of life. People who get their happiness from things always have to keep moving on from thing to thing as they pursue the latest fad and fashion. And the next one has to be bigger, glossier, faster, and newer, because the "new" really never does last.

"You're not with Deana anymore?" I asked Jerry when I saw him a few months ago. He had been telling me about this wonderful girl who was sharing his life and his apartment.

"Nah," he said. "She was sweet, a really nice girl, but she just didn't turn me on anymore, so I told her it was over."

"How did Deana take it?"

"Oh, she took it really hard. She cried a lot and said she had given me the best of herself, and didn't know what she was going to do now. But I said to her, 'Hey, look, I can't fake something if I don't feel it. It just isn't the same anymore. So get over it.'" Apparently Jerry was unable to see how grossly selfish his behavior really was.

The tenth commandment is about "thing" worship, and for Jerry, and for everyone who thinks as he does, people are "things" too. They use them for their pleasure and convenience; but as soon as the newness wears off, or the other person is no longer able to serve their purposes, they are ready to move on.

The apostle Paul says coveting is idolatry (Colossians 3:5). Both coveting and idolatry are about thing worship. But there is a difference: the second commandment (the one that speaks about idolatry) warns us not to make things more important than God. The tenth tells us that we should also not make them more important than people. It forbids us to put our selfish desires above the rights of others or to value people and things in terms of the benefit we can get from them.

Superman

Superman has been a popular figure since he first appeared in the 1930s. And why not? Faster than a speeding bullet, he leaps over tall buildings at a single bound. Furthermore, he is never wrong, never guesses, never misses, and never fails. He is the biggest, the brightest, the star, always the best there is.

Would you like to be Superman? It's easy! Just send $50 to Costume Craze of Lindon, Utah, and they will ship you a complete outfit, including a flying cape and a molded plastic chest showing immense muscles and perfectly sculpted abs.

Not many people would seriously consider wearing one of these to the office,[1] but in one way millions of people do try to live out the Superman dream in their lives.

Think of Christopher Reeve, the handsome actor who burst onto the Hollywood scene when he starred as the man from Krypton in the Superman movie that debuted in 1978. The success of the first film, *Superman,* was repeated in *Superman II, III,* and *IV,* and led to starring roles for Reeve in lots of other major films.

Along the way Reeve acquired a luxurious mansion, a private yacht, several airplanes, and a passion for sailing farther, flying higher, and pushing himself harder than anyone else. Twice he flew solo across the Atlantic. An expert sailor, he often competed in racing events. He also loved to race sailplanes and once climbed to 32,000 feet in the powerful rising air currents over Pikes Peak in Colorado. In addition, he was an expert skier, tennis player, and scuba diver.

For 10 years after making the first Superman film Reeve lived with British model Gae Exton, who bore him two children. In 1987 he dropped her and took up with the beautiful Dana Morosini, who was 10 years younger.

Christopher Reeve never wore his Superman outfit on the street, but he was convinced that a Superman lifestyle was the best for him.

While playing a cavalry captain in *Anna Karenina,* Reeve discovered yet another world to conquer—horseback riding. Before long he acquired a stableful of thoroughbreds and began regularly competing in the sport.

In May 1995 a cross-country jumping event took place in Culpeper, Virginia, and at the last minute Reeve decided to compete.

Dana was less than thrilled when she heard about it. "Chris, when are we going to spend some time together as a family?" she said to him.

"Maybe next year. Anyway, you can come along and watch me compete."[2]

So when the action started, Dana sat on the sidelines, watching her famous and dashing husband who, as always, was the star of the show, riding to enthusiastic applause from the admiring crowd.

For a man like Chris Reeve, the values of somebody like the apostle Paul must have seemed unfathomable, even bordering on lunacy. Nearing the close of a busy life of sacrifice and service, the aged apostle wrote:

"Do nothing from selfishness or empty conceit, but with humility of mind regard one another as more important than yourselves; do not merely look out for your own personal interests, but also for the interests of others" (Philippians 2:3, 4).

That is what the tenth commandment is all about. What Paul expressed in words, he illustrated with his life.

Giving and Getting

One minute the crowds at Culpeper were applauding, thrilled at the sight of the famous actor on his beautiful horse, and the next, everything changed. At the third hurdle, instead of jumping, Eastern Express abruptly, and for no apparent reason, applied the brakes and put down his head. As Chris went spiraling forward, his head struck the hurdle, and then he dived headfirst into the turf. The violence of the impact severed his spinal cord at the second cervical vertebra, just where the neck attaches to the shoulders.

In less time than it has taken you to read this, Chris Reeve went from being one of the brightest stars and top-earning actors in the world to a man who was dependent on others and on machines for every breath. From perpetual activity he went to what he later described as "the perpetual stillness."

It would be hard to imagine a greater transformation. But Reeve later said that the most important change that took place that day was a profound realignment of values and purpose for living. If you would like to contribute to the Christopher and Dana Reeve Foundation today, your money will not go for thoroughbred horses, racing yachts, or sailplanes, but on finding a cure for the thousands of people who, like Reeve, suffer spinal cord injuries each year. During the rest of his life Reeve used his fame as well as his immense creativity and money for this cause.

Not many people have the particular combination of talents and opportunities that brought wealth and celebrity to Christopher Reeve. But there are millions who, on their own level, are following the ethic he lived by. Things clutter their houses. Living beyond their means, they find themselves heavily in debt, many of them teetering on the edge of financial ruin. Harried and hurried by their get-more lifestyle, they have little time to spend with their children, and none at all for helping others or having a meaningful devotional life. It is hardly surprising that in 2005 more than 2 million people had to file for personal bankruptcy—by far the greatest number in history.

Coveting is love that is out of proportion, out of order, and out of place. It means placing our devotion where it doesn't belong, putting "things"—money, success, personal achievement—in the center of our existence, and believing that they are the foundation on which we can build happiness. "Things" become more important than people and their needs.

Like the other nine commandments, this one talks not only about specific acts but also values and attitudes. And this one, too, is not only prescriptive but descriptive—that is, it not only tells us how to behave, but describes how things should be, and reveals to us what God is like. He, above all, is the one who serves, the one who gives, with unselfish, self-sacrificing love.

As we've noted already, the apostle Paul urges us to "do nothing from selfishness or empty conceit," but "with humility of mind" "look out" not only "for [our] own personal interests, but also for the interests of others." In the next verses he reveals the source and inspiration for such an ideal.

> *"Have this attitude in yourselves which was also*
> *in Christ Jesus,*
> *who, although He existed in the form of God,*

did not regard equality with God a thing
to be grasped,
but emptied Himself,
taking the form of a bond-servant,
and being made in the likeness
of men.
Being found in appearance as a man,
He humbled Himself by
becoming obedient to the point of death,
even death on a cross"
(Philippians 2:5-8).

Jesus Christ is the supreme example for us. His was a life of humble service. He "emptied Himself" and poured Himself out on the altar of service and sacrifice. By doing so, He showed us an example of compassion for the lost, of practical love in action. This is what moves Christians and inspires their values. The closer we come to truly obeying the Ten Commandments, the closer we are to imitating His character and being like Him.

And this, after all, is their purpose.

The Conclusion of the Matter

Benjamin Franklin had a good idea. Wanting to improve himself, he sat down one day and made up a list of virtues. Then, methodical as always, he organized a careful plan for achieving them.

What would you think of applying Franklin's idea to the Ten Commandments? They really are a tremendous list of virtues, aren't they? So why not treat them as the world's oldest self-improvement manual and set to work until we can master every one of them?

The apostle Paul tells us that that was precisely the kind of religion he grew up with. He and his neighbors studied the commandments day and night and tried hard to improve themselves by obeying them down to the smallest detail.

But Paul came to see such an approach as a "ministry of death." Why? How could a sincere attempt to obey the Ten Commandments have such a negative result?

Because it made religion into a rulebook and reduced it to a matter of "letters engraved on stones" (2 Corinthians 3:7). Paul contrasted this with the "new covenant," a term he took from the prophecy of Jeremiah 31:31-33. The core of this approach is incredibly simple. It says: "I will be their God, and they shall be My people" (verse 33).

What this means is that true religion focuses not on rules but on a relationship. And it finds its center not in ourselves and our behavior but in God and His everlasting love. So rather than being a ladder that we laboriously ascend, hoping one day to climb high enough to get into heaven, the Ten Commandments become, as God intended them to be, holy principles designed to help us avoid endless suffering and foolish mistakes. They truly are a "law of liberty" (James 2:12).

Under the new covenant, the way of keeping God's law is also different, because the covenant includes a promise: "I will put My law within them, and on their heart I will write it" (Jeremiah 31:33). It is what the apostle Paul refers to when he says that believers are letters written by "the Spirit of the living God, not on tablets of stone, but on tablets of human hearts" (2 Corinthians 3:3).

Right here we have the key. That is what makes all the difference, because all this is God's work and not ours. When the center of our lives is a relationship of love with God through His Son Jesus Christ and the fellowship of the Spirit, then the Ten Commandments get off the stones and into our hearts.

Good conduct—obedience—that comes only from knowing what is right will be superficial and partial at best. But a heart renewed by the Holy Spirit will be able to offer obedience as a genuine and unselfish expression of love and gratitude to God.

And that is the invitation I leave with you at the conclusion of our review of the Ten Commandments: to enter without delay into that covenant of peace, that relationship of love. Here is God's promise to all who respond. I hope you will consider it carefully and make it your own:

"I will sprinkle clean water on you, and you will be clean. . . . Moreover, I will give you a new heart and put a new spirit within you; and I will remove the heart of stone from your flesh and give you a heart of flesh. I will put My Spirit within you and cause you to walk in My statutes, and you will be careful to observe My ordinances" (Ezekiel 36:25-27).

---

[1] Even Clark Kent doesn't wear his Superman suit to work.

[2] Christopher Reeve, *Still Me* (New York: Random House, 1988), chap. 1.

If you are interested in knowing more about this topic and other Bible-related issues:

- Visit **www.itiswritten.com** to view a weekly Bible study program online and use the free online Bible studies.

- Find answers to hundreds of Bible questions in 16 languages at **www.Bibleinfo.com.**

- Explore Bible lessons, games, and stories just for kids at **www.KidsBibleinfo.com.**

- Find more books on Bible-related topics at **www.reviewandherald.org.**

- Request Bible study guides by mail. Send your name and address to:
  DISCOVER
  It Is Written
  Box 0
  Thousand Oaks, CA 91359

Positive TV
for the Entire Family!

To order a satellite dish system call:
1-888-393-4673

Also watch Hope Channel online at:
www.hopetv.org

- Broadcasting relevant programs full of hope
- Wholesome children's programs
- Inspiring music to lift your spirit
- Health programs to reduce stress and sickness
- Inspirational teaching for successful living
- Travel to exotic lands

CHANNEL